PREFACE

This book grew out of work in General Studies with students at South-wark College for Further Education. These students were largely 16–18 year olds doing a variety of technical, commercial, and general courses on a day release or block release basis.

Approximately an hour of their day would be given to General Studies. We had found some difficulty in devising courses which corresponded to the students' interests, with some relevance to them and with a subject matter which presented some challenge.

A critical interest in their own education was common to many of these students so a detailed look at the workings of our educational system provided the stimulus for this investigation.

We would like to thank the students for their interest and forbearance; from their criticisms and insights we learned a great deal.

Our grateful thanks are also due to the Principal of the College, Norman Dark, and the Vice-Principal, Stuart Milner, for their assistance and encouragement, and to our numerous typists, particularly Lena Poidevin and Avis Field.

Frank Field
Patricia Haikin

READINGS FOR GENERAL STUDIES

TWENTIETH-CENTURY STATE EDUCATION

Edited by

Frank Field and Patricia Haikin

OXFORD UNIVERSITY PRESS 1971

Oxford University Press, Ely House, London W.1

GLASGOW NEW YORK TORONTO MELBOURNE WELLINGTON
CAPE TOWN SALISBURY IBADAN NAIROBI LUSAKA ADDIS ABABA
DAR ES SALAM BOMBAY CALCUTTA MADRAS KARACHI LAHORE
DACCA KUALA LUMPUR SINGAPORE HONG KONG TOKYO

0028856

Printed and bound in Great Britain by
Richard Clay (The Chaucer Press), Ltd
Bungay, Suffolk

ACKNOWLEDGEMENTS

The editors would like to thank the following authors or executors, and their publishers for permission to use extracts from their books.

L. J. Burrows, 'What's in Store for the Children', *The Teacher* (1967).

Alec Clegg, 'The Middle School Cometh', *The Teacher* (1967).

Margaret Cole, *What is a Comprehensive School?* (London Labour Party, 1954).

Robin Davis, *The Case for the Grammar School* (Penguin Books, 1967).

J. W. B. Douglas, *The Home and the School* (MacGibbon & Kee, J. E. Floud, A. H. Halsey, and F. M. Martin, *Social Class and Educational Opportunity* (William Heinemann, 1956).

Brian Jackson, *Streaming: An Education System in Miniature* (Routledge & Kegan Paul, 1964).

Brian Jackson and Dennis Marsden, *Education and the Working Class* (Routledge & Kegan Paul, 1961).

R. M. T. Kneebone, *I Work in a Secondary Modern School* (Routledge & Kegan Paul, 1957).

G. Lyons, 'Difficulties of a Slum Primary School', *New Society*, 1966.

S. C. Mason, 'The Leicestershire Plan' (Council and Education Press).

P. Musgrove, *The Sociology of Education* (Methuen, 1965).

The Observer, 'A School of the Future', July 1967.

John Partridge, *Life in a Secondary Modern School* (Victor Gollancz, 1966).

Robin Pedley, *The Comprehensive School* (Penguin Books, 1963).

A. Razzell, *Juniors – A Postscript to Plowden* (Penguin Books, 1968).

J. Vaizey and J. Sheehan, *Resources for Education* (George Allen & Unwin, 1968).

The editors would also like to thank the Controller of Her Majesty's Stationery Office for permission to reproduce extracts from the following:

Early Leaving Reports 1954, 1963; *Education Circular 10/65*; *Educational Reconstruction, White Paper, 1943*; *The Hadow Report, 1926*; *The Newsom Report, 1963*; *The Norwood Report, 1943*; *The Plowden Report, 1967*; *The Robbins Report, 1961*; and H. A. L. Fisher, *Introducing the 1918 Education Act*.

CONTENTS

Preface   iii
Acknowledgements   v

SECTION ONE
THE STRUCTURE AND PURPOSE OF
STATE EDUCATION   1

Background   3
H. A. L. Fisher introducing the 1918 Education Act   5
The Education of the Adolescent   7
The Three Types of Child   8
Educational Reconstruction   10
The Organization of Secondary Education   14

SECTION TWO
EXPENDITURE ON EDUCATION   17

SECTION THREE
EDUCATIONAL OPPORTUNITY   23

FAMILY — SOCIAL CLASS   25
School Class and Social Class   25
Chances of Admission to Grammar School   28
Success at Grammar School   29
Numbers Available for Higher Education (1)   33
Numbers Available for Higher Education (2)   34
FAMILY — PARENTAL MOTIVATION   38
Level of Interest   38
Limitations on Interest   40
Effect on Early Leaving   43
FAMILY-SIZE   46
Size of Family   46
LINGUISTIC DEVELOPMENT   48
Use of Language   48

ENVIRONMENT 51
   Schools in the Slums (1) 51
   Schools in the Slums (2) 53
   Living Conditions and Educational Achievement 58
STRUCTURE OF THE EDUCATIONAL SYSTEM 60
   The Stages of Primary Education 60
   Regional Inequalities in Selection 61
   Streaming 63

SECTION FOUR
THE SCHOOLS 67
THE PRIMARY SCHOOL 69
   Achievement in the Primary School 69
   Difficulties of a Slum Primary School 74
THE GRAMMAR SCHOOL 81
   The Case for the Grammar School 81
   Grammar School Values 84
THE SECONDARY MODERN SCHOOL 88
   Tribute to the Secondary Modern School 88
   Shortcomings in the Secondary Modern School 90
THE COMPREHENSIVE SCHOOL 94
   The Case for the Comprehensive School 94
   Inside the Schools 95

SECTION FIVE
NEW DIRECTIONS 101
   The Streamed and Unstreamed School 103
   The Middle School (1) 105
   The Middle School (2) 107
   The Leicestershire Plan 108
   A School of the Future 111

Index 113

THE STRUCTURE AND PURPOSE OF STATE EDUCATION

BACKGROUND

The state has taken responsibility for the education of its children for only a hundred years. Before 1870 the provision of schools had been left to private individuals and to church bodies. It was not then considered the responsibility of the state to provide schools, though every year after 1833 Parliament voted a sum of money which assisted Church of England and Nonconformist Societies to run elementary schools.

In spite of the pioneering work of these societies many districts had no school at all. In the 1850s and 1860s public interest in education grew and many people recognized the need for elementary schools for all children. The Education Act of 1870 empowered local authorities to 'fill the gaps'. Where voluntary church schools existed, these were to continue and to be subsidized by public money. Where there was no such school, a district board was to be elected by rate payers and this board was empowered to provide elementary schools. The cost was to be met by small fees (from 1d. per week to 1s. – equivalent in purchasing power to about 8d. – 8s.) and by money from a special education rate.

Competition between Board Schools and Church Schools led to rapid school building. So by 1876 it was fairly realistic to make attendance at school compulsory throughout the country for children who lived within two miles of a school, though the law could not be strictly enforced until there were enough attendance officers. In 1891 fees were abolished in most elementary schools.

At that time most people considered that elementary education was quite sufficient for the majority of children. The responsibility of the School Boards ended when a child was 10; secondary education was the responsibility of parents and independent schools, such as the old endowed grammar schools, where the classics still dominated the curriculum. Even so some school boards extended classes for children over 11 by forming 'Higher Tops' as they were usually called, and by creating 'Higher Grade Schools'. There were 70 of these with an attendance of 32,000 by 1900. So they provided what was virtually a secondary education within the elementary school system. In addition a number of schools were able to enter older scholars for grants made available by the recently created Science and Art Department. In 1899 the school-leaving age was raised to 12.

These promising developments were however cut short by decisions in 1901 by the Court of Queen's Bench and the Court of Appeal that a School Board did not possess the right to apply any portion of the school fund to a form of education which came under the control of the Science and Art Department.

There was no overall authority until the Board of Education was set up in 1899. Administrative confusion continued until the Education Act of 1902. This Act abolished the local school boards. In most cases the County Borough or County Councils were to be responsible for providing free elementary and secondary education, normally on a fee-paying basis, within their areas. The actual work was to be done by education committees whose members were elected from the Council or co-opted because of special qualifications. The voluntary or church schools became entitled to substantial rate aid from the newly created Local Education Authorities. The administrative system set up in 1902 continued to operate until it was modified by the Education Act of 1944.

The years following 1902 saw a leap forward in secondary education comparable with the rapid extension of primary education after 1870. A variety of types of schools were built. Maintained LEA secondary schools, often called 'High Schools', were patterned on grammar schools and offered a similar curriculum. Central schools in London and other big cities often 'creamed off' children at 11 from the elementary council and voluntary schools. Most children stayed in senior elementary schools which were built as separate departments on the same site as elementary schools. In country districts the all-age schools remained.

The 11 plus examination for scholarships and free places at the grammar and central schools became general after 1907; though between 1931 and 1944 parents who could afford to do so were required to contribute to school fees. In some of the bigger towns, junior technical, junior commercial and junior art schools took pupils from the age of 13 to 16.

The provision of secondary education was very uneven. The 1918 Act introduced legislation which increased the share of government contribution to education, and raised the school leaving age to 14 for all children without exemptions. It was intended that young people over 14 should attend part time day continuation schools but this reform was never implemented compulsorily.

Attitudes to the purpose and function of secondary education have been much debated during this century. The following extracts trace some of the changes in ideas.

The extract from Fisher's introductory speech to the 1918 Act shows a changing attitude on the part of the government to the purpose of education.

H. A. L. FISHER INTRODUCING THE 1918 EDUCATION ACT

There is a growing sense, not only in England but through Europe, and I may say especially in France, that the industrial workers of the country are entitled to be considered primarily as citizens and as fit subjects for any form of education from which they are capable of profiting. I notice also that a new way of thinking about education has sprung up among many of the more reflecting members of our industrial army. They do not want education only in order that they may become better technical workmen and earn higher wages. They do not want it in order that they may rise out of their own class, always a vulgar ambition, they want it because they know that in the treasures of the mind they can find an aid to good citizenship, a source of pure enjoyment and a refuge from the necessary hardships of a life spent in the midst of clanging machinery in our hideous cities of toil. I ask whether there is a single struggling young student in this country to whom a library of good books has not made an elemental democratic appeal.

> Unlike the hard, the selfish and the proud,
> They fly not sullen from the suppliant crowd,
> Nor tell to various people various things,
> But show to subjects what they show to kings.

I will now descend to our specific proposal which may be conveniently though not exhaustively, considered under six heads. Firstly, we desire to improve the administrative organization of education. Secondly, we are anxious to secure for every boy and girl in this country an elementary school life up to the age of fourteen which shall be unimpeded by the competing claims of industry. Thirdly, we desire to establish part-time day continuation schools which every young person in the country shall be compelled to attend unless he or she is undergoing some suitable form of alternative instruction. Fourthly, we make a series of proposals for the development of the higher forms of elementary education and for the improvement of the physical condition of the children and young persons under instruction. Fifthly, we desire to consolidate the elementary schools Grants, and, sixthly, we wish to make an effective survey of the whole educational provision in the country and to bring private educational institutions into closer and more convenient relations to the national system.

I now come to the most novel if not the most important provision in the Bill. We propose that, with certain exceptions to be defined in the Bill, every young person no longer under any obligation to attend a public elementary school shall attend such continuation school as the local education authority of the area in which he resides may require for a period of 320 hours in the year, or the equivalent of eight hours a week for forty weeks.

The proposal, then, comes to this, that in general young persons who are not undergoing full-time instruction will be liberated from industrial toil for the equivalent of three half-days a week during forty weeks – two half-days to be spent in school, while one will be a half-holiday.

We have reached a point in our history when we must take long views. We are a comparatively small country, we have incurred the hostility of a nation with a larger population and with a greater extent of concentrated territory and with a more powerful organization of its resources. We cannot flatter ourselves with the comfortable notion, I wish we could, that after this War the fierce rivalry of Germany will disappear and hostile feelings altogether die down. That in itself constitutes a reason for giving the youth of our country the best preparation which ingenuity can suggest. And there is another reason. We are extending the franchise, we are making a greater demand than ever before upon the civic spirit of the ordinary man and woman at a time when the problems of national life and of world policy upon which this House will be called upon to decide have become exceedingly complex and difficult, and how can we expect an intelligent response to the demands which the community propose to make upon the instructed judgment of its men and women unless we are prepared to make some further sacrifices in order to form and fashion the minds of the young.

From: H. A. L. Fisher, *Introducing the 1918 Education Act, Hansard* (H.M.S.O.).

The majority of children over 11 were still in all age elementary schools in 1926.

The Hadow Committee was set up to consider the provision of courses of study suitable for less academic children up to the age of 15. It reflects the growing interest in the nature of secondary education.

THE EDUCATION OF THE ADOLESCENT

There is a tide which begins to rise in the veins of youth at the age of eleven or twelve. It is called by the name of adolescence. If that tide can be taken at the flood, and a new voyage begun in the strength and along the flow of its current, we think that it will 'move on to fortune'. We therefore propose that all children should be transferred, at the age of eleven or twelve, from the junior or primary school either to schools of the type now called secondary, or to schools (whether selective or non-selective) of the type which is now called central, or to senior and separate departments of existing elementary schools. Transplanted to new ground, and set in a new environment, which should be adjusted, as far as possible, to the interests and abilities of each range and variety, we believe that they will thrive to a new height and attain a sturdier fibre. But we recognize that much depends on the nature of the new ground and the quality of the new environment.

From: *The Hadow Report* (H.M.S.O., 1926).

The Norwood Committee was set up to consider suggested changes in the Secondary School curriculum; this report contains one of the best explanations of the rationale behind the tripartite system of education.

THE THREE TYPES OF CHILD

The evolution of education has thrown up certain groups, each of which can and must be treated in a way appropriate to itself. Whether such groupings are distinct on strictly psychological grounds, whether they represent types of mind, whether the differences are differences in kind or in degree, these are questions which it it not necessary to pursue. Our point is that rough groupings, whatever may be their ground, have in fact established themselves in general educational experience, and the recognition of such groupings in educational practice has been justified both during the period of education and in the after-careers of the pupils.

For example, English education has in practice recognized the pupil who is interested in learning for its own sake, who can grasp an argument or follow a piece of connected reasoning, who is interested in causes, whether on the level of human volition or in the material world, who cares to know how things came to be as well as how they are, who is sensitive to language as expression of thought, to a proof as a precise demonstration, to a series of experiments justifying a principle: he is interested in the relatedness of related things, in development, in structure, in a coherent body of knowledge. He can take a long view and hold his mind in suspense; this may be revealed in his work or in his attitude to his career. He will have some capacity to enjoy, from an aesthetic point of view, the aptness of a phrase or the neatness of a proof. He may be good with his hands or he may not; he may or may not be a good 'mixer' or a leader or a prominent figure in activities, athletic or other.

Such pupils, educated by the curriculum commonly associated with the Grammar School, have entered the learned professions or have taken up higher administrative or business posts. Whether the curriculum was designed to produce men of this kind we need not enquire; but the assumption is now made, and with confidence, that for such callings a certain make-up of aptitudes and capacities is necessary, and such make-up may for educational purposes constitute a particular type of mind.

Again, the history of technical education has demonstrated the importance of recognizing the needs of the pupil whose interests and abilities lie markedly in the field of applied science or applied art. The boy in this group has a strong interest in this direction and often the necessary qualities of mind to carry his interest through to make it his life-work at whatever level of achievement. He often has an uncanny insight into the intricacies of mechanism whereas the subtleties of language construction are too delicate for him. To justify itself to his mind, knowledge must be capable of immediate application, and the knowledge and its application which most appeal to him are concerned with the control of material things. He may have unusual or moderate intelligence: where intelligence is not great, a feeling of purpose and relevance may enable him to make the most of it. He may or may not be good at games or other activities.

The various kinds of technical school were not instituted to satisfy the intellectual needs of an arbitrarily assumed group of children, but to prepare boys and girls for taking up certain crafts – engineering, agriculture and the like. Nevertheless it is usual to think of the engineer or other craftsman as possessing a particular set of interests or aptitudes by virtue of which he becomes a successful engineer or whatever he may become.

Again, there has of late years been recognition, expressed in the framing of curricula and otherwise, of still another grouping of pupils, and another grouping of occupations. The pupil in this group deals more easily with concrete things than with ideas. He may have much ability, but it will be in the realm of facts. He is interested in things as they are; he finds little attraction in the past or in the slow disentanglement of causes or movements. His mind must turn its knowledge or its curiosity to immediate test; and his test is essentially practical. He may see clearly along one line of study or interest and outstrip his generally abler fellows in that line; but he often fails to relate his knowledge or skill to other branches of activity. Because he is interested only in the moment he may be incapable of a long series of connected steps; relevance to present concerns is the only way of awakening interest, abstractions mean little to him. Thus it follows that he must have immediate returns for his efforts, and for the same reason his career is often in his mind. His horizon is near and within a limited area his movement is generally slow, though it may be surprisingly rapid in seizing a particular point or in taking up a special line. Again, he may or may not be good with his hands or sensitive to Music or Art.

Within this group fall pupils whose mental make-up does not show at an early stage pronounced leanings in a way comparable with the other groups which we indicated. It is by no means improbable that, as the kind of education suitable for them becomes more clearly marked out and the leaving age is raised, the course of education may become more and more supple and flexible with the result that particular interests and aptitudes may be enabled to declare themselves and be given opportunities for growth. That a development of this kind yet lies to great extent in the future does not preclude us from recognizing the existence of a group whose needs require to be met in as definite a manner as those of other groups.

From: *The Norwood Report* (H.M.S.O., 1943).

The 1944 Act was an attempt to organize the diversity of existing schools into a coherent scheme.

This extract from the government White Paper which immediately preceded the Act outlines the new structure. The period of compulsory school attendance was extended to 15 immediately and to 16 as soon as circumstances permitted. Education was seen as a continuous process but conducted in successive stages – the primary stages for all children up to 11; then secondary schools of equal standing but of diversified types to cater for the different needs of children as outlined in *The Norwood Report*.

EDUCATIONAL RECONSTRUCTION

General Provisions

It is intended that the raising of the school leaving age to 15, postponed in 1939, should be brought into effect as soon as possible after the war, and that provision should be made for a further extension to 16 at a later date.

It is proposed that the statutory system of public education shall cease to be severally administered for the purpose of elementary education and higher education respectively. It will be organized in three progressive stages to be known as primary education, secondary education, and further education, and a duty will be placed on each Local Authority to contribute towards the mental, moral and physical development of the community by securing the provision of efficient education throughout those stages for all persons in the area capable of profiting thereby.

Children under Compulsory School Age

Primary education covers the period up to the age of 11 or 12. For the younger children, though it is not proposed to lower the age at which attendance becomes compulsory – and no other country has a lower age than 5 – it is proposed to substitute for the present power of Local Education Authorities a duty to provide, or aid the supply of such nursery schools as in the opinion of the Board may be necessary. It is now considered that the self-contained nursery school, which forms a transition from home to school, is the most suitable type of provision for children under 5. Such schools are needed in all districts, as even when children come from good homes they can derive much benefit, both educational and physical from attendance at a nursery school. Moreover, they are of great value to mothers who go out to work, and also to those who need relief from the burden of household duties combined with the care of the young family. It is however, in the poorer parts of the large cities that nursery schools are especially necessary.

Infants and Juniors

It is generally accepted that, wherever numbers make it possible, there should be separate schools for infants and juniors respectively, because of the different methods of approach appropriate to the training of the younger and older children in the primary stage. . . . It is further an essential element in the proposals to secure a progressive reduction in the size of classes in infants' and junior schools, as the supply of teachers and buildings permits.

Secondary Education

At about the age of 11 comes the change from the junior to the senior stage. At present all children of the appropriate age and standard enter for the Special Place examination and, from what has been said previously it is clear that there is urgent need for reform. Accordingly, in the future, children at the age of about 11 should be classified, not on the results of a competitive test, but on an assessment of their individual aptitudes largely by such means as school records, supplemented, if necessary, by intelligence tests, due regard being had to their parents' wishes and the careers they have in mind. Even so, the choice of one type of secondary education rather than another for a particular pupil will not be finally determined at the age of 11, but will be subject to review as the child's special gifts and capacities develop. At the age of 13, or even later, there will be facilities for transfer to a different type of education, if the original choice proves to have been unsuitable. The keynote of the new system will be that the child is the centre of education and that, so far as is humanly possible, all children should receive the type of education for which they are best adapted.

If this choice is to be a real one, it is manifest that conditions in the different types of secondary schools must be broadly equivalent. Under present conditions the secondary school enjoys a prestige in the eyes of parents and the general public which completely overshadows all other types of school for children over 11. Inheriting as it does a distinguished tradition from the old English Grammar School it offers the advantages of superior premises and staffing and a longer school life for its pupils. Since 1902, when Local Education Authorities were first empowered to provide or aid secondary education, there has been a rapid expansion. In 1904 there were 86,000 pupils; today there are 514,000, of whom considerably more than half are in schools provided by Local Education Authorities. The success of the schools in dealing with this extension has been remarkable. The traditional curriculum has been widened and adapted to meet the ever-increasing variety of demands and, helped by the introduction in 1917 of the School Examinations system, an education has been evolved which in the main meets the needs of the more promising pupils. But in spite of this success, the schools are facing an impossible task. An academic training is ill-suited for many of the pupils who find themselves moving along a narrow educational path bounded by the School Certificate and leading into a limited field of opportunity. Further, too many of the nation's abler children are attracted into a type of education which prepared primarily for the University and for the administrative and clerical professions; too few find their way into schools from which the design and craftsmanship sides of industry are recruited. If education is to serve the interests both of the child and of the nation, some means must be found of correcting this bias and of directing ability into the field where it will find its best realization.

Compared with the grammar schools the senior schools have a recent history. Today they are one of the main elements of post-primary education. Lacking the traditions and privileged position of the older grammar school they have less temptation to be 'at ease in Zion'. Their future is their own to make, and it is a future full of promise. They offer a general education for life, closely related to the interests and environment of the pupils and of a wide range embracing the literary as well as the practical, e.g. agricultural, sides. In many areas admirable examples exist of fully developed senior schools, but they are still too few in number. The further advance of schools of this type depends on a longer school life for the pupils, a more complete reorganization, better buildings and amenities, and a more generous scale of staffing.

Junior Technical Schools came into being in 1905 and their success has been remarkable. Planned to give a general education associated with preparation for entry to one or other of the main branches of industry or commerce they have grown up in close relation to local needs and opportunities of employment. But their progress in numbers has been comparatively slow and their chances of attracting the most able children vis-a-vis the grammar schools have been adversely affected by the fact that they normally recruit at the age of 13. With altered conditions, and with a more rapid development in the future, they hold out great opportunities for pupils with a practical bent.

Such, then, will be the three main types of secondary schools to be known as grammar, modern and technical schools. It would be wrong to suppose that they will necessarily remain separate and apart. Different types may be combined in one building or on one site as considerations of convenience and efficiency may suggest. In any case the free interchange of pupils from one type of education to another must be facilitated. . . .

But laws cannot build better human beings and it is not the machinery of education so much as its content that will count in the future. Already in one direction a start has been made. Public opinion will, undoubtedly look for a new approach to the choice and treatment of school subjects after the war. In particular, consideration must be given to a closer relation of education in the countryside to the needs of agricultural and rural life and, more generally, to creating a better understanding between the people of the town and of the country. A new direction in the teaching of history and geography and modern languages will be needed to arouse and quicken in the pupils a livelier interest in the meaning and responsibilities of citizenship of this country, the Empire and of the world abroad. Education in the future must be a process of gradually widening horizons, from the family to the local community, from the community to the nation, and from the nation to the world.

From: *the government White Paper on 'Educational Reconstruction', 1943* (Cmd. 6458).

Secondary education took on another dimension with the movement to end selection at 11 and separation in secondary education.

The following is an extract from a government Circular of 12 July 1965 on the organization of comprehensive education. Local Education Authorities were not legally bound to follow this directive.

THE ORGANIZATION OF SECONDARY EDUCATION

I. *Introduction*

1. It is the Government's declared objective to end selection at eleven plus and to eliminate separatism in secondary education. The Government's policy has been endorsed by the House of Commons in a motion passed on 21 January 1965:

> 'That this House, conscious of the need to raise educational standards at all levels, and regretting that the realization of this objective is impeded by the separation of children into different types of secondary schools, notes with approval the efforts of local authorities to reorganize secondary education on comprehensive lines which will preserve all that is valuable in grammar school education for those children who now receive it and make it available to more children; recognizes that the method and timing of such reorganization should vary to meet local needs; and believes that the time is now ripe for a declaration of national policy.'

The Secretary of State accordingly requests local education authorities, if they have not already done so, to prepare and submit to him plans for reorganizing secondary education in their areas on comprehensive lines. The purpose of this Circular is to provide some central guidance on the methods by which this can be achieved.

II. *Main Forms of Comprehensive Organization*

2. There are a number of ways in which comprehensive education may be organized. While the essential needs of the children do not vary greatly from one area to another, the views of individual authorities, the distribution of population and the nature of existing schools will inevitably dictate different solutions in different areas. It is important that new schemes build on the foundation of present achievements and preserve what is best in existing schools.

3. Six main forms of comprehensive organization have so far emerged from experience and discussion:

(i) The orthodox comprehensive school with an age range of 11–18.

(ii) A two-tier system whereby all pupils transfer at 11 to a junior comprehensive school and all go on at 13 or 14 to a senior comprehensive school.

(iii) A two-tier system under which all pupils on leaving primary school transfer to a junior comprehensive school, but at the age of 13 or 14 some pupils move on to a senior school while the remainder stay on in the same school. There are two main variations: in one, the comprehensive school which all pupils enter after leaving primary school provides no course terminating in a public examination, and normally keeps pupils only until 15; in the other, this school provides G.C.E. and C.S.E. courses, keeps pupils at least until 16, and encourages transfer at the appropriate stage to the sixth form of the senior school.

(iv) A two-tier system in which all pupils on leaving primary school transfer to a junior comprehensive school. At the age of 13 or 14 all pupils have a choice between a senior school catering for those who expect to stay at school well beyond the compulsory age, and a senior school catering for those who do not.

(v) Comprehensive schools with an age range of 11 to 16 combined with sixth form colleges for pupils over 16.

(vi) A system of middle schools which straddle the primary/secondary age ranges. Under this system pupils transfer from a primary school at the age of 8 or 9 to a comprehensive school with an age range of 8 to 12 or 9 to 13. From this middle school they move on to a comprehensive school with an age range of 12 or 13 to 18.

4. The most appropriate system will depend on local circumstances and an authority may well decide to adopt more than one form of organization in the area for which it is responsible. Organizations of types (i), (ii), (v) and (vi) produce schools which are fully comprehensive in character. On the other hand an organization of type (iii) or (iv) is not fully comprehensive in that it involves the separation of children of differing aims and aptitudes into different schools at the age of 13 or 14. Given the limitations imposed by existing buildings such schemes are acceptable as interim solutions, since they secure many of the advantages of comprehensive education and in some areas offer the most satisfactory method of bringing about reorganization at an early date. But they should be regarded only as an interim stage in development towards a fully comprehensive secondary organization.

The School Community

A comprehensive school aims to establish a school community in which pupils over the whole ability range and with differing interests and backgrounds can be encouraged to mix with each other, gaining stimulus from the contacts and learning tolerance and understanding in the process. But particular comprehensive schools will reflect the characteristics of the neighbourhood in which they are situated; if their community is less varied and fewer of the pupils come from homes which encourage educational interests, schools may lack the stimulus and vitality which schools in other areas enjoy. The Secretary of State therefore urges authorities to ensure, when determining catchment areas, that schools are as socially and intellectually comprehensive as is practicable. In a two-tier system it may be possible to link two differing districts so that all pupils from both areas go to the same junior and then to the same senior comprehensive schools.
From: *Circular 10/65* (H.M.S.O., 1965).

EXPENDITURE ON EDUCATION

This extract gives some idea of the growth and distribution of expenditure on education and the proportion of the national income spent on it.

John Vaizey is Professor of Economics at Brunel University and John Sheehan is a member of the Nuffield Resources for Learning Project.

1. *In General*

During the nineteen-twenties, from 1921 to 1929, we note, expenditure varied between some £84·6 m. to £89·7 m. This constancy is a remarkable fact, suggesting how much changes in the size and composition of the child population must have affected the average *per capita* expenditure. The oscillation during the nineteen-thirties is striking by contrast with the earlier period. A peak of £95·7 m. in 1931 was succeeded by a fall to £88·7 in 1934 and then a rise to £106·3 m. in 1939. These changes are attributable mainly to price changes, as a comparison with the tables of expenditure in real terms will show. Expenditure in real terms in 1931 was greater than that at the two later dates, when indeed in real terms the outlays were almost identical although the change in money terms was considerable. The war years mark in terms of expenditure at current prices a considerable rise, but in terms of 1948 prices a considerable fall below the levels of 1939. By 1949 real expenditure was above 1938. The post-war expansion, from 1946, suggests a rise from £168·1 m. to £410·6 m. in 1955, or to more than 245 per cent the 1946 level. Over half of this rise is attributable to price changes; the remainder represents a genuine increase in real expenditure of some twice the 1938 levels, and two-thirds more than in 1946. Between 1955 and 1965, money outlays rose from £410·6 m. to £1,114·9 m. or by a further three times. By far the greater part of this rise was due to the increase in salaries and prices.

This represents a massive switch of educational expenditure towards the older age-groups and, by implication, in the direction of those with social and educational advantages. In other words, what has actually happened flies in the face of the *Newsom* and *Plowden* Reports, and supports *The Robbins Report*.

TABLE 1

Expenditure in Real Terms on Public Education in the United Kingdom, 1920 to 1965

Year	Expenditure £m. at 1948 prices	Index
1920	100·2	47
1925	141·3	66
1930	152·9	71
1935	158·4	74
1938	165·0	77
1940	154·9	72
1945	144·6	67
1948	215·3	100
1950	263·0	122
1955	300·0	141
1965	451·4	210

2. Spending in the Different Sections

Table 2 illustrates the distribution of government expenditure since 1920.

TABLE 2

Public Education Expenditure in Different Uses (at 1948 prices) in the United Kingdom, 1920 to 1965

	1920	1930	1938	1948	1953	1955*	1965*
Primary	42·8	42·6	39·5	31·9	30·0	30·7	21·1
Secondary	17·7	18·7	23·0	21·4	21·1	22·3	28·0
Further	6·0	5·2	5·5	4·7	6·2	6·0	12·7
Special	1·4	1·5	1·9	1·0	1·4	1·5	1·7
Meals and milk	1·2	2·7	3·6	7·8	10·6	10·8	5·1
Health	1·2	1·8	2·3	3·7	1·9	1·9	1·0
Training of teachers	0·4	0·3	0·3	1·7	1·4	1·3	3·4
Admin. and insp.	4·7	4·6	3·6	5·4	5·1	3·8	3·2
Universities	5·2	5·9	6·7	7·9	8·5	8·2	9·9
Scotland	17·9	14·9	11·9	12·4	11·0	11·0	11·3
Northern Ireland	1·5	1·7	1·7	2·0	2·6	2·4	2·5
Total	100	100	100	100	100	100	100

* At current prices.

3. As a Proportion of the National Income

It may be noted that in the nineteen-twenties the proportion of the national income usually devoted to public education was 2·2 per cent. In the boom of 1921 it was higher than this, and in 1930 it was a little higher, too. By the slump year of 1932 the proportion had risen to 2·5, and it remained at about 2·4 until the rising national income of the late nineteen-thirties overtook the expansion of education, and reduced the proportion to 2·2 per cent, again in 1939. During the war years the proportion sank rapidly to 1·5 per cent in 1944, and the early years of the Labour Government were devoted to raising the proportion to what it had been in 1933. By 1951, the year when Mr. Attlee's Government was defeated at the polls, the proportion had risen to 2·7 per cent. The next year there was a slight fall, but then the percentage settled down to a steady 2·8 per cent. From then, until 1965, the proportion rose dramatically to 4·1 per cent.

These figures are changed and reinforced by including capital expenditure. The early years of the period are scarcely affected by the inclusion of the small amounts of capital expenditure then undertaken, but by 1930 the total had risen to some 2·7 per cent (instead of 2·3 per cent), and then sank to about 2·5 per cent in the middle nineteen-thirties, before rising to 2·7 per cent again in 1938. Thereafter the figure sank as capital investment was rigorously cut, until the school building programme began again in 1946. By 1950 the percentage was 3·1 (instead of 2·7), and by 1955 the percentage had risen to about 3·4 per cent (instead of 2·8). By 1965, the proportion has risen to 5·4 per cent, or exactly twice the proportion that education took of the national income in 1938.

From: John Vaizey, John Sheehan, *Resources for Education* (George Allen & Unwin, 1968).

EDUCATIONAL OPPORTUNITY

FAMILY–SOCIAL CLASS

The bearing of social class on the placing of children in streamed classes in junior schools is examined in this article. The extract is taken from Brian Jackson's study of streaming in primary schools in which he compares ten streamed schools, academically and socially, with ten unstreamed schools.

Mr. Jackson is now Director of the Advisory Centre for Education and helped set up the National Extension College. His research was done for the Institute of Community Studies, an independent research organization.

SCHOOL CLASS AND SOCIAL CLASS

Having examined the extent of the streaming principle, and the variety of methods that lead up to an 'A', 'B', or 'C' grading, we can stand back a little and look for other factors at work. If the individual class teacher were asked about the 'A', 'B', 'C' divisions he might reply that

TABLE 1

11-year-old children: Fathers' Occupation in 140 Two-stream Schools

Fathers' occupation	'A' stream	'B' stream	Total %
Professional and managerial	73%	27%	100%
Clerical	61%	39%	100%
Skilled manual	56%	44%	100%
Semi-skilled manual	42%	58%	100%
Unskilled manual	39%	61%	100%
Percentage of children in each stream	53%	47%	100%
Total number of 11-year-old children sampled	5,285		

the very able children were placed in the 'A' stream, the average ones in the 'B' stream, and the below average ones in the 'C' stream. But can we isolate other things that these children have in common so as to illuminate what 'very able', or 'B' or 'below average' mean?

One obvious factor is social class. The teachers were therefore asked to give the father's occupation. (Allowing for some inaccuracy of reporting by the teachers) the returns from 140 two-stream schools are set out in Table 1.

Streaming placed the middle-class child in the 'A' rather than the 'B' stream, and this was also true (though only just) of the skilled manual group.

The same pattern was found in the three-stream school. In Table 2 the chances of Professional parents' children entering the lowest of the three streams are only 14 in a 100; and again the skilled manual group is slightly on the more favoured side, leaving the largest percentages of the children of semi-skilled fathers in the 'B' class and of unskilled fathers in the 'C'.

TABLE 2

11-year-old children: Fathers' Occupation in
252 Three-Stream Schools

Fathers' occupation	'A' stream	'B' stream	'C' stream	Total
Professional and managerial	58%	28%	14%	100%
Clerical	47%	32%	21%	100%
Skilled manual	41%	35%	24%	100%
Semi-skilled manual	29%	41%	30%	100%
Unskilled manual	21%	34%	46%	100%
Percentage of children in each stream	37%	36%	27%	100%
Total number of 11-year-old children sampled	14,200			

The four-stream school displays the same trend; every extension of streaming increases the above-average chances of the young middle-class pupil:

TABLE 3

11-year-old Children: Fathers' Occupations in
228 Four-Stream Schools

Fathers' occupation	'A' stream	'B' stream	'C' stream	'D' stream	Total %
Professional and managerial	55%	17%	13%	5%	100%
Clerical	40%	32%	17%	11%	100%
Skilled manual	34%	30%	24%	12%	100%
Semi-skilled manual	20%	28%	31%	21%	100%
Unskilled manual	14%	24%	30%	32%	100%
Percentage of children in each stream	30%	28%	25%	17%	100%
Total number of children sampled	7,097				

In the four-stream school, the professional or manager's child has 95 chances in a 100 of not being in the 'D' stream, whereas a third of the labourers' children end up there, even though the numbers in this school class are relatively small. Once a mixed ability group is divided into an 'A' and 'B' stream, the professional man's child takes 20 per cent more than his numerical 'share' of 'A' stream places. If they are divided into 'A', 'B', 'C', and 'D' groups he claims 25 per cent more. And once more the rough-and-ready 'class' line between clerical and skilled manual is blurred a little, leaving the semi-skilled and un-skilled as a distinct group whose children move chiefly into the lower streams. These analyses illustrate the considerable reinforcement of social differences created by primary school streaming.

From: Brian Jackson, *Streaming: an education system in miniature* (Routledge & Kegan Paul, 1964).

This study of the relation between social class and success in gaining grammar school places is part of an investigation carried out under the auspices of the Department of Sociological and Demographic Research at the London School of Economics. The three sociologists began their study in 1952 taking their samples from two contrasting areas, a prosperous part of Hertfordshire and a less prosperous town in Yorkshire.

CHANCES OF ADMISSION TO GRAMMAR SCHOOL

The proportion of the 10–11 age-group of children in each occupational group selected for admission to grammar schools give what may be called the 'class-chances' of a grammar school education.

The following are the figures for boys in 1953 in South-West Hertfordshire and Middlesborough:

	South-West Hertfordshire	Middlesborough
	%	%
Professional workers, business owners and managers	59	68
Clerical workers	44	37
Foremen, small shopkeepers, etc.	30	24
Skilled manual workers	18	14
Unskilled manual workers	9	9
All	22	17

As might be expected, there were in both areas considerable disparities in the chances of boys from different social classes. In general, the sons of manual workers had a chance below the average, and the sons of non-manual workers a chance above the average, of being selected for grammar schools. The sons of clerks had four or more times as good a chance as the sons of unskilled manual workers, and two to three times the chance of sons of skilled workers. The difference in chances at the extremes of the occupational scale was still greater. In Middlesborough the son of a professional or business man had more than seven times the chance of the son of an unskilled worker, and almost five times the chance of a skilled worker's son, while in South-West Hertfordshire he had three times the chance of the skilled worker's and six times that of the unskilled worker's son.

From: J. E. Floud, A. H. Halsey and F. M. Martin, *Social Class and Educational Opportunity* (William Heinemann, 1956).

The Report of the Minister of Education's Central Advisory Council considered what factors influence the age at which boys and girls leave secondary schools which provide courses beyond the minimum school-leaving age. The report is notable in retrospect for its presentation of the evidence of the influence of social class on school performance.

This extract considers the influence of social background on the achievement of children at grammar schools.

SUCCESS AT GRAMMAR SCHOOL

The great majority of boys and girls can be classified according to the nature of their fathers' occupations; and armed with this knowledge of circumstances which reflect the social background, we can see what relation it has both to the chances of admission to a grammar school and to a successful career in it.

TABLE 1

Occupational Background of Pupils of Maintained and Direct Grant Schools

	Fathers' occupation					
	Professional and managerial %	Clerical %	Skilled %	Semi-skilled %	Un-skilled %	
All schools	(15)	(4)	(51)	18	12	100
Grammar schools	25·0	10·3	43·7	15·3	5·6	100
Sixth forms	43·7	12·0	37·0	5·8	1·5	100

The figures in the top line are calculated from the 1951 Census returns; the other figures are derived from our sample. The comparison leaves little doubt that by the time the local education authorities hold their allocation examination at 11 the children of certain social groups have as a whole begun scholastically to outstrip those at the other end of the scale, and that the same process is continued among those selected from grammar schools during their time there. . . .

If the figures shown in the two lower lines of Table 1 were all the evidence about the performance at the grammar school of children with differing social backgrounds, it might mean no more than that the same boys and girls who had done best in the selection test at 11 continued to excel in their passage through the school and, since there already were more of them from professional and managerial homes than from unskilled workers' it would not be surprising to find that the proportion staying on for sixth form work was higher.

However, many pupils who do well at 11 do less well at 16 and vice versa. Table 2 analyses this by parental occupations.

TABLE 2

Comparison of Pupils' Achievements at beginning and end of their Grammar School life (Maintained Grammar Schools only)

Selection group at 11	Academic category at 16–18	Professional and managerial %	Clerical %	Skilled %	Semi-skilled %	Un-skilled %
1.	A B C	79·9	64·6	60·1	46·8	29·6
	D	10·2	16·8	13·6	15·4	16·3
	E F	9·9	18·6	26·4	37·9	54·0
	All	100	100	100	100	100
2.	A B C	61·8	53·3	42·6	27·7	25·6
	D	12·8	15·2	16·5	14·6	12·0
	E F	25·4	31·5	40·9	57·7	62·4
	All	100	100	100	100	100
3.	A B C	48·3	36·3	32·6	22·8	12·8
	D	18·2	21·5	15·6	15·1	10·7
	E F	33·5	42·2	51·8	62·1	76·4
	All	100	100	100	100	100

It will be seen that the improvement between 11 and 16 which has raised many pupils from the bottom selection group to the highest academic categories is most common (amounting to 48·3 per cent) among those from professional and managerial occupations, while the corresponding deterioration which has caused many who were placed in the top selection group at 11 to be found by 16 in the lowest academic categories is most common among the children of unskilled workers (54·0 per cent) and semi-skilled workers (37·9 per cent). There are, of course, plenty of pupils whose fathers are of professional or managerial standing who were in the lowest selection group at 11 and are still in the lowest categories at 16. Similarly, among the children of semi-skilled or unskilled workers 46·8 per cent and 29·6 per cent respectively of those who were in the top selection group at 11 were also in the highest academic categories at 16–18.

Table 2 is concerned solely with actual academic achievements. It might perhaps be suggested that the poor showing of children from the homes of un- and semi-skilled workers was caused largely by their family tradition being against a long school life and certainly against a sixth form career; that if they had not had a high proportion of very early leavers their academic performance might have been similar to that of other social groups. Table 3, however, shows how closely the schools' estimate of their pupils' capacity follows the general pattern of Table 2.

TABLE 3

Comparison of Pupils' Achievement at Beginning and Schools' Estimate of Capacity at End of School Life (Maintained Grammar Schools only)

Selec-tion group	Best suited for course leading to:	Fathers' occupation				
		Professional and managerial %	Clerical %	Skilled %	Semi-skilled %	Un-skilled %
1.	Two advanced subjects	70·8	55·6	46·6	34·0	21·0
	General sixth	12·6	15·7	14·5	11·7	16·8
	Ordinary level only	16·7	28·7	38·9	54·3	62·1
	All	100	100	100	100	100
2.	Two advanced subjects	42·0	33·5	26·4	13·0	15·5
	General sixth	20·2	11·9	14·9	12·1	7·3
	Ordinary level only	37·7	54·5	58·6	74·9	77·2
	All	100	100	100	100	100
3.	Two advanced subjects	26·1	20·2	17·1	9·3	4·7
	General sixth	21·9	12·5	12·2	9·2	4·7
	Ordinary level only	51·9	67·4	70·7	81·5	90·6
	All	100	100	100	100	100

The figures in Tables 2 and 3 show unmistakably how often home background influences the use which a boy or girl will make of a grammar school education. In our analysis we have been concerned only with broad classifications, and we are well aware that many individual children of well-to-do parents find little support at home for hard work at school and academic ambition, while many children from very poor homes have parents who know the worth of the education they themselves missed. Still it is beyond doubt true that a boy whose father is of professional or managerial standing is more likely to find his home circumstances favourable to the demands of grammar school work than one whose father is an unskilled or semi-skilled worker. The latter is handicapped. . . .

One of the significant findings to which we wish particularly to call attention concerns the children of semi-skilled and unskilled workers. Of the 1,621 children in our sample who entered the grammar school from these two classes, 917, or more than half, failed to get as many as three passes at Ordinary level, and of these 520 left before the end of their fifth year. 32 per cent, and 37 per cent, respectively of the failures in these two ways, compared with 21 per cent, of the whole entry, were from these types of homes. Our sample tells us, therefore, that of approximately 16,000 children who in 1946 entered grammar schools throughout England from such homes, about 9,000 failed to get three passes at Ordinary level and of these about 5,000 left before the end of their fifth year.

So many of the unskilled workers' children achieved little that it will be worth while considering them separately. The first point to observe is the low rate of entry from the unskilled workers' home. The number of children from unskilled workers' families who might have been found in our grammar school sample if the proportion were the same as in the population as a whole is about 927; the actual number was 436. This suggests that some 5,000 children from unskilled workers' homes who might have been expected, if the yield from unskilled workers' homes were the same from other homes, to enter grammar schools in England in 1946, did not qualify for admission. The second important finding is the high rate of academic failure among those who did. Of the 436 children admitted 284, or two-thirds, left without as many as three passes at Ordinary level. Thus, of about 4,360 children from unskilled workers' homes who entered grammar schools, only about 1,500 obtained the benefit that the grammar school is especially designed to give. At a higher level the wastage was even more marked: on the same calculation only 230, or one in twenty, obtained two Advanced passes or entered for two Advanced subjects. These represent 1·4 per cent of the 17,000 children who took advanced courses, about one-ninth of the proportion in which unskilled workers' children are found in the population as a whole.

From: *Early Leaving Report* (H.M.S.O., 1954).

Starting from the premise that higher education should be available for all who wanted it and were qualified for it, *The Robbins Report* reviewed the pattern of full-time higher education in Great Britain. The report revealed both a considerable demand for higher education and a pool of ability as yet not fully exploited. The two extracts show how the pattern of University entry is linked to that of social background.

NUMBERS AVAILABLE FOR
HIGHER EDUCATION (1)

Not only has there been less redistribution of opportunity in secondary education since 1944 than is generally assumed but such as has taken place has not gone beyond the threshold of the Sixth Form. The evidence suggests that the striking growth in the numbers of qualified candidates for higher education represents in large measure the response of the non-manual classes to current social and economic pressures, and that the effects of democratizing policy in secondary education have yet to make themselves fully felt in higher education. The proportion of grammar school pupils and of university students coming from working-class homes has grown considerably, the percentage of all children at this social level who pass into the grammar schools and universities remain small; and changes in the 'class chances' of admission to these institutions have been much less striking than might appear from the familiar changes that have taken place in their social composition. The proportion of the annual age-groups of working-class boys passing into the grammar schools increased by 50 per cent after the war, but on the most recent information the figure is still very low – rather less than one in six as compared with nearly one in two of those from non-manual homes. At the university level, the chances of working-class boys are apparently virtually unchanged, although those of boys from other families have more than doubled. Only one working-class boy in fifty proceeded to the universities in the later post-war period, for which we have information, as compared with one in five boys from other families. It seems that in higher education we still await the sons and daughters of manual workers who, since the war, have been drawn into the grammar and comparable schools, but have not so far crossed the threshold of the Sixth Form in representative strength.

From: 'Higher Education', *The Robbins Report* (H.M.S.O., 1961).

NUMBERS AVAILABLE FOR HIGHER EDUCATION (2)

One of the purposes of this survey was to throw light on the factors affecting the achievement of school children and their entry to higher education. The Crowther Report had already indicated the close asso-

TABLE 1

Percentage of Children Born in 1940–1 reaching
Full-time Higher Education: by Father's Occupation
Great Britain

Percentage

	Full-time higher education		No full-time higher education	All children	Numbers (= 100%)
	Degree-level	Other			
Father's occupation					
BOYS *Non-manual* and					
GIRLS Higher Professional	33	12	55	100	15,000
Managerial and other professional	11	8	81	100	87,000
Clerical	6	4	90	100	38,000
Manual Skilled	2	2	96	100	248,000
Semi- and unskilled	1	1	98	100	137,000
BOYS Non-manual	15	4	81	100	70,000
Manual	3	2	95	100	189,000
GIRLS Non-manual	9	10	81	100	70,000
Manual	1	2	97	100	196,000

ciation between a father's level of occupation and the educational achievement of his children at school. As Table 1 shows, our survey confirmed that the association with parental occupation is, if anything, still closer where higher education is concerned. For example, the proportion of young people who enter full-time higher education is 45 per cent for those whose fathers are in the 'higher professional' group, compared with only 4 per cent for those whose fathers are in skilled manual occupations. The underlying reasons for this are complex, but differences of income and of the parents' educational level and attitudes are certainly among them. The link is even more marked for girls than for boys.

Clearly the economic circumstances of the home are very influential: even in families of the same occupational level the proportion of children reaching full-time higher education is four times as high for children from families with one or two children as from those where five or more children have claims on the family's resources. Thus a continuing growth in family incomes is likely to increase still further the demand for higher education. There is also a very important influence from the educational background of the parents (although this is, of course, related to their social class or occupation). As Table 2 shows, the proportion reaching full-time higher education is eight times as high among children whose fathers continued their own education to

TABLE 2

Percentage of Children Born in 1940–1 Reaching Full-time
Education: by Father's Age on Completing Full-time Education
Great Britain

Percentage

	Full-time higher education		No full-time higher education	All children	Numbers (=100%)
	Degree-level	Other			
Father's age on completing full-time education					
18 or over	32	11	57	100	22,000
16 or 17	14	7	79	100	41,000
Under 16	2	3	95	100	491,000

the age of eighteen or over as among those whose fathers left school under sixteen. These facts suggest that, just as since the war more children have stayed on at school for a full secondary education, so in turn more of their children will come to demand higher education

TABLE 3

Percentage of Leavers from Maintained Grammar Schools having Two or more Passes at Advanced Level: by Grading in 11+ and Father's Occupation England and Wales 1960–1

Percentage

	Percentage of leavers of all ages who have 2 or more 'A' levels	Percentage of leavers of all ages who leave aged 18 and over	Percentage of leavers aged 18 and over who have 2 or more 'A' levels
	(1)	(2)	(3)
GRADING IN 11+			
Father's occupation			
Upper third			
Professional and managerial	57	55	79
Clerical	44	39	74
Skilled manual	38	40	77
Semi- and unskilled	21	23	81
Middle third			
Professional and managerial	33	42	63
Clerical	18	29	56
Skilled manual	18	27	59
Semi- and unskilled	10	15	58
Lower third			
Professional and managerial	14	32	43
Clerical	16	22	58
Skilled manual	10	18	51
Semi- and unskilled	4	7	53
Transfer from secondary modern school	15	29	49
ALL GROUPS AT 11+			
Professional and managerial	37	46	67
Clerical	26	32	64
Skilled manual	22	29	65
Semi- and unskilled	11	17	56
All children	24	31	65

during the 1970's. The desire for education will tend to spread as more and more parents have themselves received a fuller education.

There is impressive evidence that large numbers of able young people do not at present enter higher education. Table 3 gives some of the results of a recent Ministry of Education survey of school leavers which, at our request, was extended to provide information on parental occupation and on performance at the age of eleven. Column 1 shows that, of grammar school leavers with a given measured ability at the age of eleven, the proportion obtaining the qualifications for entry to higher education varies widely according to their social background. Children of manual workers are on an average much less successful than children of the same ability in other social groups. This is largely because they leave school earlier. A comparison of Columns 1 and 2 of the table shows that the proportion of children of manual workers who stay on to the age when the General Certificate of Education at Advanced level is normally attempted is smaller than the proportion of middle class children who actually achieve two passes at Advanced level. But as may be seen from Column 3 of the table those children who do stay on are on average as successful as children of the same ability in other social groups.

While the reserves of untapped ability may be greatest in the poorer sections of the community, this is not the whole of the story. It is sometimes imagined that the great increase in recent years in numbers achieving good school-leaving qualifications has occurred almost entirely among the children of manual workers. This is not so. The increase has been almost as great among the children of professional parents, where the pool of ability might have been thought more nearly exhausted. In these groups the performance of children of a given measured ability has in fact continually improved. The desire for education, leading to better performance at school, appears to be affecting children of all classes and all abilities alike, and it is reasonable to suppose that this trend will continue.

From: 'Higher Education', *The Robbins Report* (H.M.S.O. 1961).

FAMILY–PARENTAL MOTIVATION

The following articles examine the effect of parental encouragement of children in school.

In the first article the level of interest of the parents was partly based on comments made by the class teachers at the end of the first and at the end of the fourth primary school year, and partly on the records of the number of times each parent visited the schools to discuss their child's progress with the Head or class teacher. Parents are said to show a 'high level of interest' if the teachers regarded them throughout the primary school period as very interested in their children's work and if they had also taken the opportunity to visit their primary schools at least once a year to discuss their children's progress. They show a 'fair level of interest' if they fall short on one of these counts, and a 'low level of interest' if they fall short on more than one.

J. W. B. Douglas is Director of the Medical Research Unit at the London School of Economics.

LEVEL OF INTEREST

The middle-class parents take more interest in their children's progress at school than the manual working-class parents do, and they become relatively more interested as their children grow older. They visit the schools more frequently to find out how their children are getting on with their work, and when they do so are more likely to ask to see the Head as well as the class teacher, whereas the manual working-class parents are usually content to see the class teacher only. But the most striking difference is that many middle-class fathers visit the schools to discuss their children's progress, whereas manual working-class fathers seldom do so. (Thirty-two per cent of middle-class fathers visit the schools, but only 12 per cent of manual working-class fathers.) The teachers' contacts with the working-class families are largely through the mothers, and this may explain why they become relatively less frequent as the children get older, whereas with the middle classes they become more frequent. The working-class mothers have a particular interest in seeing how their children settle in when they first go to school, but may feel diffident about discussing their educational progress with the teacher at a later stage; and it seems either that their husbands are not prepared to take on this responsibility or that they are unable to do so owing to the difficulty of taking time off work to visit the schools. . . .

So far then we have seen that those parents who are most interested in their children's education come predominantly from the middle classes, and those who are least interested from the manual working class. Within each social class, however, the parents who give their children most encouragement in their school work also give them the best care in infancy. The manual working-class parents show this more strongly than the middle-class parents; if they show a high level of interest in their children's school work, then their standards of care and their use of the services are also high, and they have middle-class standards too in their views on the school-leaving age and in their expectations of grammar school awards. . . .

As one would expect children do relatively well in the secondary selection examinations if their parents take much interest in their work and relatively badly if they take little interest. This difference is most marked in the manual working classes, where 40 per cent of the former go to grammar schools and only 10 per cent of the latter. The teachers, though more optimistic than the results of the 11 + examinations justify, take a similar view and consider that 59 per cent of the manual working-class children are suitable if their parents are interested, and only 15 per cent if they are uninterested. In the middle classes also the teachers' views show a similar agreement with the results of secondary school selection and the level of parents' interest.

The children with parents who are interested in their work do well in the secondary selection examinations and are favourably rated by their teachers largely because they are of superior measured ability at eleven. Once this factor is allowed for, they still have a slight additional advantage in the examinations; those with very interested parents get 10 per cent more places than we would expect, whereas those with un-interested parents get 7 per cent fewer. It is, however, the children at the borderline of the level of ability needed for grammar school entrance, who get substantially more grammar school places if their parents are interested in their work; they get 19 per cent more places than expected whereas those with uninterested parents get 14 per cent fewer.

From: J. B. W. Douglas, *The Home and the School* (MacGibbon & Kee, 1964).

Brian Jackson and Dennis Marsden studied the school careers of 88 working-class children in a northern industrial city. This extract shows the parents' reactions to their children's grammar school education.

LIMITATIONS ON INTEREST

In the first two years of grammar school there were very few parents who were not touched by the excitement of knowledge in some way. Parents who had not opened a book for years began to read their children's set texts, and fathers settled down to maths and physics homework alongside their sons and daughters. Whereas the middle-class child looked to his parents for help with homework, there was here rather a co-operation in learning. . . .

After a year or two the children's natural respect for their parents lay uneasily alongside their own clearer mastery of the new skills, and alongside many other doubts that school and early education promoted. There was the beginnings of a split, or at least of a growing sense that the child was out on his own, moving into worlds to which the parents had no access.

But as such awareness began to develop, as the school and its work took on unexpected turns and became both more demanding and important to the child, many of the parents sought to reassert control over their children's education by demanding some clear statement about the kind of job this was leading to. And this voice was generally the father's. . . . the fathers often found it hard to see what kind of training it was that the grammar school offered when technical and commercial subjects found no place on the timetable. To what end all this history and geography, French and Latin? It all seemed to contradict their often 'technical college' vision of education and to lead only into misty nothingness.

By the third and fourth year questions about future jobs were becoming insistent. This was of course the age at which the parents themselves had taken their first jobs, and it seemed unnatural to some that a boy or girl had not yet come to terms with the future. There was more than one voice suggesting at this stage that perhaps a commercial or a strictly technical course might have been better, might have been surer than the grammar school. And it was perhaps natural that there should be this early anxiety about a job, from men and women who knew only too well how much secure work mattered. Besides this, some of the parents badly needed that their children manifestly succeed in life, where they had made so little impression themselves: and for almost all there were the neighbours whose embarrassing sceptical questions could be so hard to answer.

'Many a time you'd be out and the neighbours would say, "EEh, is your lad still at school? What's he going to be then?" and I'd have to say, "I don't know what he's going to be yet." And they'd say, "Doesn't he know yet?" and then I'd come home and I'd sit opposite our lad in the chair and I'd say "What do you think you'll be when you leave school?" "I don't know, I don't know, don't bother me," he'd say and that was it. When the neighbours bothered me, I hadn't got an answer and I felt soft. They'd look at you as much as to say, "staying on at school all that time and don't know what he is going to be, well!"'

Most children were as unsure of the future as their parents, and as uninformed about possibilities. By the age of 15, only a small minority of our sample had made some decision (not always realized) about a future job. How was it that the number was so small, and how was it that so many of the parents did not get more advice?

Clearly the obvious place to get this was the school. The schools usually offered an annual opportunity for parents to consult teachers, and of course it was always possible to make an appointment with the head. Yet it was clear indeed that these opportunities were only taken up by the more prosperous, and by some of those who had grammar school experience themselves. And even in these groups it was often only one parent who visited the school. Many families made only sporadic contact with the staff, sometimes giving up after the early years; and there were a handful of instances in which neither parent had ever visited the school. . . .

Only very rarely could this be put down as simple neglect. We asked the parents why they did not go to school more, and their answers were so various, and sometimes so barely sensible as to be merely sketchy rationalizations. Some said they were always working late or the bus journey was a difficult one – despite the fact that their children had managed it daily since the age of eleven. Others felt their attendance would upset the child, others still reported how uncomfortable they felt in the presence of the teachers and further parents. Some felt that one visit a year was worse than no use at all, and complained of the hurry and the big crowds on that night. Others again spoke of the teachers as not being interested in them or their children.

No doubt many of these charges are unfair. But some of these statements made more sense than others and ran true to the rest of the interview. There was for instance no doubt why these parents so seldom belonged to the formal parent-teacher organizations. These groups were run, and often very ably run, by professional-class parents and it was sheer social discomfort that kept working-class parents at a distance. There was no bad feeling over this, rather it was recognized that in a sense the school 'belonged' more to the professional parents and it was only natural that they should also 'own' the parent-teacher body. Besides they clearly did the work well and gave generously of their time and talents. But this feeling of intruding into an alien world 'belonging' to others, spread over the whole school, hindering the interested and worried parents and hardening the few careless and idle ones.

. . . so to many, the education of their children seemed to be slipping away from their control. To begin with there had been their own rediscovery of the delights of learning and, in a sense, some began the grammar school course alongside their children. But after the first years came the worrying doubts and frank ignorance about what it might lead to, and when the reassurances and the knowledge did not flow back from the school, a dormant father might awake into a more sceptical life. Those families in which the aspirations were very strong continued to encourage their children to adapt themselves to a new kind of life, and they were not too depressed by unfamiliar problems in their relationships to child or school. They were pleased by the newly acquired polish, and had some sense of what the future held. Parents below the top fringe of the working class were much more bewildered by the to-and-fro relationship with their children, and by their general lack of contact with school and future. By the time the leaving age was reached) the General Certificate taken, many wondered whether there was much to be gained by leaving their child at school. And cutting right across all categories was that small group of parents fiercely living out their own ambitions through their children, and tolerating no obstacles to their path.

The end of the 'O' level course was a moment for pausing for reconsidering the whole venture – even in the case of highly gifted children. This of course is the point at which very large numbers of working-class children abandon the grammar schools.

From: Brian Jackson and Dennis Marsden, *Education of the Working Classes* (Routledge & Kegan Paul, 1962).

The extract from the *Early Leaving Report* considers the influence of parents in determining the age at which the child leaves school.

EFFECT ON EARLY LEAVING

One of the main influences must be sought in the outlook and assumptions of parents and children in various walks of life. Consider first the outlook of parents in professional occupations. Most of them have had a grammar school or similar education, and others have made their way into a position in society in which they find such a background taken for granted. They all engaged on work for which a fairly high level of education is an obvious advantage and many follow professions to which a specified educational standard is a condition of entry. In the circumstances is not surprising if they assume that their children will not leave school at 15 but will stay as much longer as their ability justifies. This assumption is not necessarily due to any conscious sense of the value of education; it may be a mere social convention which has never been questioned. But it is in any case a powerful influence on the parents towards keeping their children at school, and on the children towards staying.

Most of the parents whose occupations are described as skilled, semi-skilled and unskilled will themselves have left school at 14. It does not of course follow that they will lack a sense of the value of education; indeed this sense may be more keenly felt by a man who is conscious of what he has missed than by anyone else. But inevitably the continuance of full-time education to the age of 16, 17 or 18 cannot be taken for granted by such parents as it is by most parents of professional standing; and if it is not taken for granted by the parents it will not be by the children. Thus children in different groups may start their grammar school life with different sets of unspoken assumptions about the length of school life. Similarly their fathers' varying occupations cannot fail to influence their first assumptions about their own careers.

But ideas are picked up not only in the home, but in the neighbourhood. It is easy to imagine, for instance, that a headmaster may despair of keeping in the sixth form any boy from a particular street, not only because of the poor conditions in the houses but because of the character and atmosphere of the street as a community. There is no doubt of the strength of the pressure on even conscientious parents from neighbours who see no point in education beyond 15 or 16 as the case may be. If the pressure on the parents is strong it is much stronger on the children.

The decision to leave may well be the child's and not the parents'. We tried in all our questionnaires to find out how often it was one rather than the other. From the answers given it was seen that the schools thought the parents responsible twice as often as the children, but one of the strongest impressions received was of decisions to leave made by the girls and boys themselves; they often answered that their parents did not mind one way or the other and left the decision to them. It does not follow, of course, that in such cases the home influence is negligible; in this context neutrality on the part of parents is likely to tell in favour of leaving, since ephemeral irritations and ambitions may well be uppermost in an adolescent mind. It should be the function of the parents to look further ahead.

The trends illustrated here are even more marked for girls than boys. It seems that far more boys than girls left for career reasons and rather more because they found school work difficult; more girls than boys left because they found the restraints of school life irksome and because their families could not afford to keep them at school longer, and rather more because their friends were leaving. This suggests that petty irritation with school is commoner among girls than boys and that parents are not prepared to make sacrifices so readily for their daughters as for their sons.

This is not surprising. It is common knowledge that many parents attach more importance to their sons' education than to their daughters'. The idea is not dead that a good education is wasted on a girl because she will get married, and if a choice seems necessary between taking a boy or a girl away from school it is usually the girl who leaves. If the mother dies, falls ill or is overworked, a girl may be brought home to look after the family. Some light is thrown on the respective attitudes of parents in different walks of life by a comparison of the figures shown for boys and girls in Table 1.

It will be seen that at the sixth form level boys are found in the majority in all groups. Among the earliest leavers there is a marked preponderance of girls everywhere except in the professional and managerial group. This suggests a difference of social convention about the level of education necessary for girls and may indicate the critical

TABLE 1

Length of School Life: Boys compared with Girls

Academic categories (grouped to show length of school life)	Father's occupation									
	Professional and managerial		Clerical		Skilled		Semi-skilled		Un-skilled	
	Boys	Girls	Boys	Girls	Boys	Girls	Boys	Girls	Boys	Girls
	%	%	%	%	%	%	%	%	%	%
A and B (sixth form leavers)	46·8	41·1	30·9	27·0	23·3	18·1	12·7	6·7	7·2	6·1
C, D, and E (fifth form leavers)	46·0	52·5	61·0	57·5	60·4	59·1	62·6	59·6	55·0	51·4
F ('premature leavers')	7·1	6·4	8·2	15·5	16·4	22·9	24·7	33·7	37·8	42·5
	100	100	100	100	100	100	100	100	100	100

stages in the school life of girls with different social backgrounds.
From : *Early Leaving Report* (H.M.S.O., 1954).

FAMILY—SIZE

The sociologists who studied the impact of social class on educational opportunity in Hertfordshire and Yorkshire found that the actual size of family had some effect on children's success at school.

SIZE OF FAMILY

Size of family is a factor which in both areas is inversely related to success in the selection examinations (Table 1). It cannot be regarded simply as a feature of the material environment of homes, although it obviously has important economic implications. In the first place, it is a well-established fact that, for whatever reason, children from large families score less well on the average in intelligence tests than children from small families even at the same social level. Moreover, it is noteworthy that the inverse relationship of success to size of family was much less marked for the children of Catholic families in Middlesborough despite the fact that the fathers of some three-quarters of these large Catholic families were unskilled workers.

However that may be, we find that in South-West Hertfordshire, 17 per cent of the children of unskilled workers with families of only one or two children were successful, as compared with 2 per cent of those whose families numbered five or more. In Middlesborough the corresponding figures for the non-Catholic unskilled workers were 9 per cent and 3 per cent respectively. Among the children of skilled workers in South-West Hertfordshire the proportion of awards to the group drawn from families of only one or two (21 per cent) was almost twice as great as to that drawn from families of three or four (12 per cent). In Middlesborough the corresponding figures for the children of non-Catholic skilled workers were 19 and 12 per cent respectively, and for children of even larger families of five or more at this social level the proportion of awards was only 5 per cent.

TABLE 1
Awards of Grammar School Places in Relation to Family Size

	Percentage awarded grammar school places. No. of children in family		
	1–2	3–4	5+
South-West Hertfordshire (1952)			
Middle and lower middle class	35 (255)	31 (169)	21 (42)
Working class: skilled	21 (277)	12 (245)	17 (108)
unskilled	17 (122)	11 (126)	2 (64)
All	26 (654)	18 (540)	13 (214)
Middlesborough (1953)			
Middle and lower middle class	43 (103)	28 (71)	20 (20)
Working class: skilled	19 (115)	12 (133)	5 (75)
unskilled	9 (86)	7 (109)	3 (87)
All	24 (304)	14 (313)	6 (182)

From: J. E. Floud *et al.*, *Social Class and Educational Opportunity* (William Heinemann 1956).

LINGUISTIC DEVELOPMENT

Basil Bernstein has undertaken a research project at the London Institute of Education into the speech characteristics of middle- and working-class children and the possible effect this could have on their educational progress.

The following is a summary of his findings.

USE OF LANGUAGE

Bernstein has worked with middle- and working-class boys in London and found that in the working-class sub-culture there is on the whole a particular mode of speech that is characterized by its very restricted nature. Sentences are short, dependent clauses are few, vocabulary is small, adjectives few and not used with fine discrimination, abstract ideas are rarely used, and finally gesture is commonly used in addition to or in place of speech. This syntactically simple language may be called 'restricted code', and those who are brought up to speak this code will automatically be brought to think in the same uncomplicated way regardless of whether they are genetically capable of far more complex thought. To those who can use a more complex code of speech there will not be the same limit to mental development. In the middle-class sub-culture children hear the speech of their parents and imitate it. This tends to be a more elaborate mode of speech; sentences are long, and contain a complicated structure of dependent clauses, many subtly chosen adjectives are used, the words 'it' and 'one' are common, abstract nouns are found, and gesture assumes a much less important place in communication. This is termed 'elaborated code' and gives its speakers the possibility of thinking of a much more complex and abstract quality than is open to those who speak in restricted code. The middle-class child can understand both codes, but the working-class child is brought up to a restricted code and finds great difficulty in translating elaborated code into something that he can understand. It should perhaps again be added that the account given here for ease of exposition covers limiting cases. Between these limits there will exist combinations of the two extremes.

Evidence for this theory is provided by examining the results of members of the working and middle classes in intelligence tests. Bernstein gave a verbal and non-verbal test to two groups. The first consisted of 61 Post Office messenger boys aged fifteen to eighteen, none of whom had been to a grammar school. This group could be safely considered as working class. The second group was made up of 45 boys from a major public school who were matched for age with the first group. This was the middle-class group. For the working-class group the results on the verbal test clustered around an IQ of 100, whereas on the non-verbal test thirty-six out of sixty-one had an IQ greater than 110. For the middle-class group the results on both tests were all above an IQ of 100 and the distribution of results in the two tests were closely matched. If the mean scores were extrapolated for a mean age of sixteen, then the difference on the non-verbal test between the two groups was 8–10 points of IQ, but it was 23·24 points on the verbal test; that is, it was more than twice as great as for the non-verbal test.

To summarize, the language scores of the working-class group were depressed in relation to the scores at the higher ranges of the non-verbal test, but this was not the case for the public-school group. It would seem that the mental operations necessary to do non-verbal tests are available to both the working and the middle classes, but that the mental operations necessary for the understanding of the more complex parts of the verbal tests are only available to the middle class and have not become a part of the mental equipment of the working class. Two things follow: Firstly, purely because of differences in social class learning the middle class have more facility in the mental operations necessary to pass the verbal intelligence tests mainly used for entrance to grammar schools, but, secondly, there must be many working class children who have high innate mental ability, but who can not have this potential developed since the mode of speech they learn in their sub-culture is of too restricted a nature to furnish them with the mental equipment that is necessary and that they could have possessed. No firm answer can be given in the present state of psychological knowledge to the question of how late a child may delay the development of his innate potential mental capacity and not damage his chances of ultimately catching up.

Therefore the working-class child may well come to school with a twofold handicap. His innate intelligence is under-developed in certain aspects that are important for success in our educational system as it is now organized, and his personality is so structured that he is unlikely to do well at school. . . . The working class child has not had his spare time carefully organized for him, as is often the case with the middle class children. He has a very general notion of the future and is incapable of pursuing long-term goals. . . . To such children arbitrary luck rather than rigorously planned work appears to be the reason for success. On the other hand the middle-class child comes to school with his intelligence developed in the direction required for success. In addition his personality has been moulded in a very different social setting so that he sees the importance of long-term goals and perceives that he himself, rather than good fortune, is the main influence on his chances of achieving such goals. . . .

Social class learning results in the school learning situation appearing very different to each social class. Clearly communication will be difficult between those who tend to speak and to think in different codes. It has been pointed out that the stress on the transmission of an elaborated code and on the moral code associated with the middle class may be perceived by a working-class child as an implicit criticism and devaluation of his own background. Yet the working-class child may come to feel unease at his failure at school, the responsibility for which may well not be his own. If we consider actual school subjects, it will probably be in his English lessons that the working-class child will most feel that his teacher is trying to change his code of speech, his method of thought and even his mode of perception. His whole system of communication seems to be under attack. Difficulties will occur in mathematics; mechanical operations, such as addition and multiplication, will be within his grasp, but the transfer of these operations to symbols that is involved in algebra could cause trouble. . . .

. . . in the world of the school all . . . is not so clear cut. . . . The situation is blurred by the existence of 'illiterate' middle-class parents who care little for their children and do not provide an environment favourable to their full development and also of working-class parents who perhaps through extensive further education have come to value education and who can speak in both codes.

From: P. Musgrave, *The Sociology of Education* (Methuen, 1965).

ENVIRONMENT

The adverse effect of a poor environment on educational opportunity is shown in the two extracts which follow.

The first is taken from the Report of the Minister of Education's Central Advisory Council, 'Children and their Primary Schools', which, under the chairmanship of Lady Plowden, considered primary education and its transition to secondary education.

SCHOOLS IN THE SLUMS (1)

In the neighbourhood where the jobs people do and the status they hold owe little to their education it is natural for children as they grow older to regard school as a brief prelude to work rather than an avenue to future opportunities. Some of these neighbourhoods have for generations been starved of new schools, new houses and new investment of every kind. Every-one knows this; but for year after year priority has been given to the new towns and new suburbs, because if new schools do not keep pace with the new houses, some children will be unable to go to school at all. The continually rising proportion of children staying on at school beyond the minimum age has led some authorities to build secondary schools and postpone the rebuilding of older primary schools. Not surprisingly, many teachers are unwilling to work in a neighbourhood where the schools are old, where housing of the sort they want is unobtainable, and where education does not attain the standards they expect for their own children. From some neighbourhoods, urban and rural, there has been a continuing outflow of the more successful young people. The loss of their enterprise and skill makes things worse for those left behind. Thus the vicious circle may turn from generation to generation and the schools play a central part in the process, both causing and suffering cumulative deprivation.

We have ourselves seen schools caught in such vicious circles and read accounts of many more. They are quite untypical of schools in the rest of the country. We noted the grim approaches; incessant traffic noise in narrow streets; parked vehicles hemming in the pavements; rubbish dumps on waste land nearby; the absence of green playing spaces on or near the school sites; tiny play grounds; gaunt looking buildings; often poor decorative conditions inside; narrow passages; dark rooms; unheated and cramped cloakrooms; unroofed outside lavatories; tiny staff rooms; inadequate storage space with consequent restriction on teaching materials and therefore methods; inadequate space for movement and P.E.; meals in classrooms; art on desks; music only to the discomfort of others in an echoing building; non-soundproof partitions between classes; lack of smaller rooms for group work; lack of spare room for tuition of small groups; insufficient display space; attractive books kept unseen in cupboards for lack of space to lay them out; no privacy for parents waiting to see the head; sometimes the head and his secretary sharing the same room; and sometimes all round, the ingrained grime of generations.

We heard from local education authorities of growing difficulty in replacing heads of similar calibre. It is becoming increasingly hard to find good heads of infant or deputy heads of junior schools. We are not surprised to hear of the rapid turnover of staff, of vacancies sometimes unfilled or filled with a succession of temporary and supply teachers of one kind or another. Probationary teachers are trained by heads to meet the needs of their schools but then pass on to others where strains are not so great. Many teachers able to do a decent job in an ordinary school are defeated by these conditions. Some become dispirited by long journeys to decaying buildings to see each morning children among whom some seem to have learned only how not to learn. Heads rely on the faithful, devoted and hard working regulars. There may be one or two in any school, or they may be as many as half the staff, who have so much to do in keeping the school running that they are sometimes too tired even to enjoy their own holidays.

We saw admission registers whose pages of new names with so many rapid crossings out told their own story of a migratory population. In one school 111 out of 150 pupils were recent newcomers. We heard heads explain, as they looked down the lines that many of those who had gone were good pupils, while a high proportion of those who had been long in the school came from crowded, down-at-heel homes.

From: 'Children and their Primary Schools', *The Plowden Report* (H.M.S.O., 1967).

The Minister of Education asked the Central Advisory Council for Education to advise him on the education of pupils aged 13 – 16 of average and less than average ability. The council was under the chairmanship of Mr. John Newsom.

The report stressed inequalities in educational provision and called for action to remedy such conditions as described in the extract.

SCHOOLS IN THE SLUMS (2)

These are the districts where, as Mr. J. B. Mays puts it,

'We find many different kinds of social problems in close association: a high proportion of mental illness, high crime and delinquency rates; and above average figures for infant mortality, tuberculosis, child neglect and cruelty. Here, too, the so-called problem families tend to congregate. Life in these localities appears to be confused and disorganized. In and about the squalid streets and narrow courts, along the landings and stairways of massive blocks of tenement flats which are slowly replacing the decayed terraces, outside garish pubs and trim betting shops, in the light of coffee bars, cafes and chip saloons, the young people gather at night to follow with almost bored casualness the easy goals of group hedonism.'

What does it feel like to be responsible for a school serving such an area?

We asked the heads of schools included in our survey to write freely about their problems. This is some of what they had to tell us.

From London

The neighbourhood presents a sorry picture of drab tumbledown dwellings in narrow mean little streets, relieved by open spaces made recently by the demolition experts, and the dreary bomb sites that have served as rubbish dumps since the last war. Overcrowding still persists in the remaining slum dwellings where people of all nationalities compete for shelter. The homes of our children are in a deplorable condition. Damp and badly maintained, many of them are overcrowded. Large families live in two or three rooms. Toilet requirements are inadequate, giving rise to difficulties through too much sharing. Slowly the Council building scheme is providing new dwellings in the blocks of flats that are now beginning to rise near the school.

From the Midlands

The school is situated alongside a large sauce and pickle factory, and there is also a large brewery just behind it. The odours of vinegar and beer are constantly present and the air is full of soot particles. Many congested streets converge on the school buildings, the houses in these streets being tightly packed in terraces and courts. They are mainly of the back-to-back variety and accommodation usually consists of one room down, in which the whole family lives, plus TV, and two to four bedrooms upstairs.

From Yorkshire

The estate was built a generation ago to house the people of the first slum clearance areas of the city. It forms a pocket about one mile from the city centre. The area has no shopping centre, recreation centre or community centre of its own. Gardens are a good reflector of the attitude and outlook of householders. Here it is obvious that few take any interest whatever in the appearance of the garden. Fences (iron) were removed during the war and that may be a contributory factor in the dilapidated condition of most.

From Yorkshire again

The area has an exceptionally high deposit of industrial dirt. The school itself has for neighbours two works within twenty yards of the playground wall, and three more within a radius of 200 yards. A railway and a canal are also within 50 yards of the school. Houses are terraced in dirty and badly illuminated streets and most are due for demolition. This has, in fact, already started in some streets in which a number of uninhabited houses offer tempting opportunities for mischief. Only one to two per cent of the houses have indoor sanitation and 36 per cent a hot water supply. . . . A large proportion of fathers spend their working life in an atmosphere of heat, dirt, noise and mechanical violence. Communication can only be carried out by shouting and the effects of this can be noticed in the home, in the street and in places of entertainment. There is, therefore, a great tendency for boys to shout at each other in ordinary conversation.

From the Midlands

The children live in back-to-back houses which are badly designed, badly lit, and have no indoor sanitation – four or five families share one public toilet in the middle of the yard. Few of the children living here have ever seen a bathroom, and in some houses there is not even a towel or soap. Canals and railway lines run alongside the houses giving bad smells, grime and smoke and noise. All these homes have over-crowded living and sleeping quarters, for example, ten or eleven people may sleep in two beds and one cot. The living room usually measures about 10ft by 9ft. and combines gas stove, cupboard, sink and small table. The children are restricted to playing in the small yard or the pavement of the main road.

From Lancashire

The homes are nearly all tenement flats, erected a generation back, or maisonettes or multi-storey flats built within the last four or five years. Almost all the dwellings are well kept by their own standards, though some of the housecraft ideas are sketchy. A growing number have wash-in machines in the £80 to £100 class on H.P. All, of course, have TV. Amongst the girls there is still an obvious need for personal hygiene, even at the level of clean necks and brushed hair for school. Some of the mothers make startling objections to school complaints of head lice, fleas, body odour, etc. Nevertheless, there is a great improvement on pre-war standards.

In the slums as everywhere else, there are good, bad and indifferent schools. No doubt the failure of a bad school in a slum is more total and more spectacular than in a middle-class suburb because of the lack of parental and community support to bolster up the industry and moderate the behaviour of the pupils. But we have no reason to suppose that bad schools are more frequent in slums than elsewhere.

What about the schools themselves? Forty per cent of all the modern schools in our sample had buildings which must be condemned as seriously inadequate. The corresponding figure for the slums is 79 per cent. Two illustrations may be given of what 'seriously inadequate' means. The first is a typical example; the second is worse than typical but by no means unique. They have been chosen because these schools happen to have the best attendance figures in this special slum group. The fact that their attendance is up to or above the average for all modern schools, shows how devotion can overcome difficulties.

A boys' school of 284 pupils

Average attendance 91·5 per cent. A very old building with nine large classrooms. In addition there is an art and light craft room. There is a library, but it is smaller than a normal small classroom, and a laboratory, but it can only take 20 boys at a time. There is a very small hall without a stage but no gymnasium, dining room, medical room, or, indeed, any other special room. Two outside centres provide between them nine sessions of woodwork per week, in addition to what is done in one woodwork room at school. A playing field is being provided for this and neighbouring schools, but was not in full use at the time of the survey. All school matches have had to be played on opponents' grounds. There is an old swimming bath (70ft. by 30ft.) ten minutes away without facilities for diving. Three sessions of 40 minutes are available per week – insufficient for all who wish to swim.

A girls' school of 209 pupils

Average attendance 93.0 per cent. A very old building with seven classrooms of 480 sq. ft. each, one of which is at present used for art and music as there is no teacher for the seventh class. Four are separated by moveable wood and glass partitions. There is no hall, gymnasium, dining room, or special room of any kind. There is a small roof playground, very exposed to wind and weather, but no fixed P.E. equipment. Netball is played in the courtyard of nearby tenements. Science has to be based on one corridor cupboard. There is a sink, gas and electricity. There are good cupboards, ironing boards, sewing machines and a fitting corner in one classroom. There is no room for light crafts. Class libraries and subject libraries are kept in portable infant type cupboards. There is sufficient time allocation at a housecraft centre to give the 2nd, 3rd, and 4th years one session per week. Four forms each week are able to visit an L.E.A. playing field half an hour away by bus. There is a very old swimming bath with poor accommodation near the school which is available for one hour per week (2 classes).

Conditions such as these must inevitably have an adverse affect on staffing. As far as the actual ratio of teachers to pupils is concerned these schools are no worse off than the general run: indeed many of them have a marginal advantage. But all our evidence stresses the need for continuity of teaching and stability in staffing. The heads of schools in the slums have nearly all pointed out in their evidence the value of teachers who are now meeting the second and even the third generation of pupils from the same family. But beside the need for such men and women who have won a place in the tradition of the neighbourhood there is an equally great need for what may be called short-term stability – that is to say stability over the period of a pupil's school life. It is this stability which we have tried to measure in our survey.

How many teachers who were in the schools in 1958, when the pupils in the survey were admitted, were still there in 1961? How many had come and gone in the interval? How much bigger was the staff in 1961? The following table answers these questions taking the 1958 staff as a 100.

	Men		Women	
	All schools	Schools in slums	All schools	Schools in slums
1958 staff still there in 1961	64	52	50	33
Teachers who came since and have stayed	50	42	61	68
Teachers who came and went	27	82	44	65

The true situation is probably even worse than these figures since a slight ambiguity in one question led some schools to underestimate the number of transients – small wonder, then, if boys and girls eyeing a new teacher are doubtful whether he will stay long enough to make it worth their while to settle down and really work for him. In these slum schools there was only an even chance that a woman who joined the staff later than the beginning of the Christmas term in 1958 would still be there in September 1961; for men the odds were two to one against. Only a third of the women and half the men had been on the staff for more than three years.

Four other ways in which schools in slums fall markedly below the general run follow as almost inevitable consequences from poor staffing and poor premises. First, very few boys and girls want to extend their compulsory school life by even one or two terms. Secondly, the less able pupils spend more of their time in ordinary classroom work than in other modern schools. In only 10 per cent of the schools in slums compared with 21 per cent of all modern schools, do the less able pupils spend roughly half or more of their time on 'practical subjects', including physical education. Thirdly, only one in eight fourth year pupils belong to school clubs or societies compared with one in four in modern schools generally. Lastly, homework is much less common in schools in slums. Sixty-nine per cent of the fourth-year boys and 59 per cent of the girls get no regular homework compared with 49 per cent of the boys and 43 per cent of the girls in modern schools as a whole.

From: 'Half Our Future', *The Newsom Report* (H.M.S.O., 1963).

This extract from the *Early Leaving Report* considers the effect of physical conditions within the home.

LIVING CONDITIONS AND EDUCATIONAL ACHIEVEMENT

We are not here concerned simply or even mainly with difference of income, although in a very broad sense the respective groups of parents' occupations into which our sample is classified represents different ranges of income the correspondence is far from exact. For example, it would not be easy to say how the incomes of parents in the clerical group compare with those of the skilled and semi-skilled workers respectively; and while the parents of professional or managerial standing will on the whole be better off than the members of any other group there will be among them, such as clergymen and teachers, of whom this is not true. We cannot assume, therefore, that the differences revealed in the performance of children in the several occupational groups are primarily attributable to differences in parental income.

At the same time, we do not underrate the effect of bad living conditions. Unhappy and broken homes, family quarrels, and lack of sound home discipline can be found in all walks of life and at all levels of society and they will always tend to have the gravest effect on school work. So will the physical conditions of the home. A child's chances at a grammar school may be very seriously impaired by bad housing or over-crowding, the absence of suitable space for study, inadequate lighting or heating, lack of quiet, the constant distraction of the wireless or television, or other forms of disturbance. In the 55,000 households shown by the 1951 census as having an average of more than three persons per room the difficulties of a grammar school child may well be overwhelming. The 300,000 households with an average of more than two persons per room are likely to provide a most unsatisfactory background. The 750,000 households with an average of $1\frac{1}{2}$ to two persons per room will also impose undue strain on a grammar school child. This number of over one million congested households is likely to be playing an important part in the problem we are studying.

We have not been able to make any inquiry into the conditions under which grammar school children do their homework. A survey which was carried out on Merseyside in 1948 found that conditions varied a good deal between winter and summer. About 4 per cent of the children did without a fire in winter in order to work alone, but in summer nearly a quarter used their bedrooms and 41 per cent, compared with 16 per cent in winter, were able to work alone. Less than half of them could say that they did not hear the wireless at all and one in eight heard it all the time. The survey concluded that in summer 27 per cent and in winter 44 per cent of the children were working under definitely bad conditions.

It is clear then that a grammar school child may be seriously handicapped by physical conditions at home. But the difference between the records of children in the respective occupational groups is too marked and too widely spread to be accounted for mainly by such conditions. Another distinction which we have tried to draw is between children whose mothers are and are not at work; but on this point the schools so often had no information, particularly about children who had left, that the evidence is inconclusive.

From: *Early Leaving Report* (H.M.S.O., 1954).

STRUCTURE OF THE
EDUCATIONAL SYSTEM

This section shows how the actual method of the organization of schools may give rise to inequality.

The extract from *The Plowden Report* examines the effect the date of birth may have on a child's educational chances.

THE STAGES OF PRIMARY EDUCATION

Children are born every day of the year. In England they are admitted to infant schools at intervals of four months (most countries have one yearly intake), and promoted to junior schools or classes only at intervals of twelve months. They must go to school at the beginning of the term after their fifth birthday; they are promoted to the junior school (or junior classes) in the September following their seventh birthday.

TABLE I

Compulsory Education in Infant Schools under Present Arrangements

Month of Birth	Year 1			Year 2			Year 3			Junior school
	Age of child in autumn term	Age of child in spring term	Age of child in summer term	Age of child in autumn term	Age of child in spring term	Age of child in summer term	Age of child in autumn term	Age of child in spring term	Age of child in summer term	Length of infant schooling on promotion
Sept.–Dec.	—	5	5	5 to 6	6	6	6 to 7	7	7	8 terms
Jan.–April	—	—	5	5	5 to 6	6	6	6 to 7	7	7 terms
May–Aug.	—	—	—	5	5	5 to 6	6	6	6 to 7	6 terms

Table 1 shows that:

There is a considerable difference in age and in the length of time children have been at school when they are promoted to the junior school. Either annual admissions, or termly promotions, would remove one or other of these differences; it is the combination of the two which imposes a double difference. . . .

Disadvantages of Termly Entry

There is evidence both from our witnesses and research that children born in the summer, who are younger and have a shorter time at school than others before they are promoted, tend to be placed in the 'C' stream of those junior schools which are organized in this way. A study of streaming found that 'the A streams had the highest average age and the lowest ability streams the youngest'. The difference persists. One county borough has found that a high proportion of the pupils born between September and December gained grammar school places compared with those born between May and August. The latter often have to transfer to junior school before they have finished learning to read. Their new teachers, not always realizing their relatively late start, may believe them to be slow learners, expect less of them and often in consequence get less from them. The 'age allowances' made in selection procedures cannot offset their phychological handicap.

From: 'Children and their Primary Schools', *The Plowden Report* (H.M.S.O., 1967).

J. W. B. Douglas examines the connection between the varied distribution of grammar school places and the measured intelligence of 11 year old children.

REGIONAL INEQUALITIES IN SELECTION

The proportion of children going to grammar schools varies from one local education authority to another: in some authorities places are given to more than 30 per cent of children, in others to less than 10 per cent. These differences, as the Ministry of Education points out, do not necessarily imply unequal opportunities for secondary education. When, as in some areas, there are many private schools, the demand for grammar school places may be low. Moreover the academic ability of children may vary in different parts of the country and so may their parents' views on the value of a grammar school education. We may also, when making the broad classification of schools into 'grammar' and 'other', fail to do justice to the opportunities provided in technical schools, to the variety of extended courses provided in secondary modern schools, and to the existing arrangements for the transfer of late-maturing pupils from secondary modern schools to grammar schools. . . .

The regional pattern is little altered when all selective places are taken into account, i.e. when children at independent and technical schools are included with those at grammar schools; and even when the children at comprehensive schools which are not conveniently streamed are added, the regional equalities persist, and are as follows:

Percentage of Children in Grammar, Technical, Comprehensive and Independent Schools

Region

Wales	South-West	North-West	West and East Ridings	East
33·5	35·0	29·5	25·6	24·6

Region

North Midland	Midland	London and South-East	North	South
26·3	24·1	31·6	22·4	18·9

It seemed possible that some of the inequalities in grammar school allocation might be explained by chance factors which could have led, for example, to a high proportion of middle-class children being selected by a heavy survey in some areas and a low one in others. There are indeed great regional differences in the occupations followed by the survey children's fathers, but they are not of the sort to explain the unequal distribution of grammar school places. The largest proportion of semi-skilled and unskilled manual workers' children is in Wales where grammar school places are in good supply; the largest proportion of professional and salaried workers' children is in the South, where there are few places available. By the token of the fathers' occupations, therefore, the existing allocation of places in these two regions should be reversed.

A similar conclusion is reached when we look at the eleven-year test scores; the Welsh children score slightly below the national average, and the children in the South slightly above it. When put into order running from the highest average measured ability to the lowest, Wales comes ninth out of the ten regions and the South comes fifth. These figures plainly give no support for the view that the regions with a high proportion of children at grammar schools have a high average level of ability and those with a low proportion at grammar schools, a low one. There seems indeed to be no consistent relation between the provision of places and the ability of children as measured by us.

There might, of course, be oddities in the distribution of measured ability that would justify the patchy and apparently illogical provision of grammar school places observed in different parts of the country, and we can exclude this possibility only by comparing the allocation of grammar school places in the different regions to children of similar measured ability. This calculation shows that if the existing grammar school places were fairly distributed throughout the country in proportion to the measured ability of the children, the chances of getting a place would be equal (18 per cent) for Welsh children and those in the Southern Region. In fact, 29 per cent of Welsh children go to grammar schools as compared with only 13 per cent of children in the South. Less extreme differences are found between the other regions.
From: J. W. B. Douglas, *The Home and the School* (MacGibbon & Kee, 1964).

In the same book Douglas looked at the effect of streaming in two-stream junior schools. He separated out a group of children who were streamed by ability before their eighth birthday and who had stayed in the same school from then until they sat the 11-plus examination. During these years they continued to be streamed by ability into one or other of two classes.

STREAMING

It was rare for children to change streams; over the whole three-year period the annual rate of transfer was 2·3 per cent and approximately the same numbers moved up as down. On this showing the system of streaming by ability is more rigid than is generally realized; for example, when, in another study, teachers in three-streamed schools were asked to estimate the proportion of pupils who were promoted or demoted, they gave on the average a figure of 19 per cent changes each year, which is more than seven times as large as the rate of change recorded in the present survey. The schools themselves also tended to give higher figures; in the same study, returns from 27 three-stream primary schools showed an average annual rate of transfer of 6 per cent. Perhaps there are more transfers in three-stream than in two-stream schools, or perhaps in these three-stream schools children who left or joined late were confounded with those who changed their streams. . . .

At each level of ability the children in the upper streams improve their scores while the others deteriorate. In the upper streams it is particularly the children of relatively low ability who benefit – those, for example, with scores between 41 and 51 improve by an average of 4·5 points, whereas those with scores between 52 and 60 improve only 1·3 points. In the lower streams, the brighter children show a greater average deterioration in test score (2·7 points) than the duller children (0·9 points). It seems then, that the less able children in the upper streams are stimulated by high standards of teaching or by the competition of brighter children, whereas in the lower streams the relatively bright children are handicapped either by unsuitable teaching or lack of competition. The figures which are given in the following table suggest why transfers between streams are so rare; once allocated, the children tend to take on the characteristics expected of them and the forecasts of ability made at the point of streaming are to this extent self-fulfilling.

| | Stream | |
| | Upper | Lower |
Measured ability at eight years	Change in score 8–11 years	Change in score 8–11 years
41–45	+ 5·67	− 0·95
46–48	+ 3·70	− 0·62
49–51	+ 4·44	− 1·60
52–54	+ 0·71	− 1·46
55–57	+ 2·23	− 1·94
58–60	+ 0·86	− 6·34

(+ = improvement   − = deterioration)

The expressed intention of the teachers was to stream these children according to their measured ability, but in the early years at primary school it seems that judgements of ability are influenced by the types of home. It is, of course, expected that there would be a greater proportion of middle-class children in the upper than in the lower streams, because of their higher average measured ability. The inequalities observed are, however, greater than this for even when children of the same level of ability are considered, the middle-class children tend to be allocated to the upper streams and the manual working-class children to the lower ones (there are 11 per cent more middle-class children in the upper streams than would be expected from their measured ability at eight years and 26 per cent fewer in the lower). . . .

The few children who moved from the lower to the upper streams are distinguished by having received superior care in early childhood, by being of higher measured ability at eight and by improving their test performance between eight and eleven years (0·95 points) as compared with a deterioration of 0·49 points observed among the children who remained in the lower streams. The children who start in the upper streams and end in the lower tend to be those from large families who received poor care in early childhood; their average score at eight years was nearer to that of children in the lower streams than in the upper and although they improved their scores between eight and eleven years by 0·15 points, this is less than a quarter of the improvement recorded for the pupils who remained in the upper streams throughout. While the reallocation of streams reinforces the original selection by ability, it also in a minor way continues the selective process which favours the children who are well cared for in early childhood. . . .

In summary, streaming by ability reinforces the process of social selection. Children who come from well-kept homes and who are themselves clean, well clothed and shod, stand a greater chance of being put in the upper streams than their measured ability would seem to justify. Once there they are likely to stay and to improve in performance in succeeding years. This is in striking contrast to the deterioration noticed in those children of similar initial measured ability who were placed in the lower streams. In this way the validity of the initial selection appears to be confirmed by the subsequent performance of the children, and an element of rigidity is introduced early into the primary school system.

From J. W. B. Douglas, *The Home and the School* (MacGibbon & Kee, 1964).

THE SCHOOLS

THE PRIMARY SCHOOL

The primary school has seen some of the most exciting experiments in education since 1945.

This extract illustrates the achievements of some such schools. It is taken from a book which is both a tribute to the achievement of many teachers in primary schools and also an indictment of the Government's failure to implement the recommendations of *The Plowden Report*.

Arthur Razzell is lecturer in child development at the University of London Institute of Education.

ACHIEVEMENT IN THE PRIMARY SCHOOL

The first school is housed in a new single-storey building situated in a pleasant, wooded area. The classrooms are light and spacious, each one equipped with water, sinks, stock-room and a plentiful supply of storage cupboards and book cases. The rooms all open out on to the playing fields and playgrounds. The school hall is equipped for use as a gymnasium and the playground contains more climbing frames and agility apparatus. An active and affluent parent-teacher association has worked with the local authority in providing additional material for the school. Consequently it lacks little in the way of modern audio-visual aids and other equipment. For some years the school has been able to make good use of a large swimming pool built and paid for by the parents.

Despite the national shortage of teachers this school has no staffing problem. The headmaster is fortunate not only in having a choice of staff when a vacancy occurs, but in being able to employ a number of part-time teachers to give additional help with small groups of children. Having the opportunity to select his teachers, he is able to choose those especially interested in working informally with groups of children of mixed intellectual ability and who will work well in a team seeking to carry out his educational aims for the school. The teachers follow no set time-table, nor are they issued with a detailed scheme of work to be carried out. Continuity is achieved by a close liaison between the teachers, and the headmaster spends much of his time working with the children in the classroom.

The school is situated in an extremely affluent area, and this might well have led to a clash between parents' ambitions for their children's academic success and the headmaster, who places considerable emphasis on keeping the school free from examination pressures. That no such antagonisms have developed is probably due to a number of factors. Firstly, the head works hard to establish and maintain good relationships with parents. He is aided in this by his very real ability to communicate exactly what the school is seeking to achieve. Secondly, he is supported by an excellent team of well-qualified teachers who enjoy working in a free and informal situation, and who are able to achieve outstandingly good results (30 to 40 per cent of the children go on to selective grammar schools). Thirdly, the school is surrounded by a number of private schools, where the emphasis is much more on academic studies of a formal nature, which cater for those preferring such methods.

The school is constantly alive with changing displays of work. On my last visit the children in one class were writing their own travel guide to the Continent, and their booklets were delightfully illustrated with drawings, diagrams, photographs and other material collected from the countries concerned. Each child was writing about a country which he had personally visited, and the sustained high quality of the work over many pages was most impressive. In mathematics the headmaster had produced a variety of useful aids, some of which are now commercially manufactured and used in many schools throughout the country.

When we consider the work achieved by these children we have to take into account their home background, the well equipped, delightful school environment, their teachers working with a common aim, and the fact that so many of them are highly intelligent youngsters.

About an hour's drive from this building stands the second school. It was built some years before the Boer War, and although massive slum clearance is taking place all around, the school remains unchanged. The classrooms are small and surrounded with those dark brown, glazed bricks commonly found in older public lavatories. The rooms are heated with open coke fires, and although the grate with its heavy iron surround takes up much of the limited space, the glowing fires add some cheer to the dark rooms on winter days. Nothing can change the prison-like confines of the architecture, and it appears more restrictive now than when I first knew it, since tall blocks of flats have largely replaced the old tenement buildings. On one side, the small playground looks out over the ruins of a deserted and derelict factory. Only one classroom has a tap and sink. It is an area where many mothers regard hair curlers, bedroom slippers and an apron as normal rig-of-the-day for visiting the school.

The young headmistress radiates charm, energy and vitality. To every new teacher who comes to work at the school she gives a pamphlet that says:

'In formulating our educational aims we must bear in mind the social background of our children. The neighbourhood provides a background quite anti-pathetic to the proper growth of children, physically, mentally or emotionally. Their surroundings give them little opportunity to do the things that children love doing – no open spaces for play; no water except that of the gutter; no gardens, but instead the overcrowded forecourt of huge blocks of flats. With such environmental conditions children from even good homes would find themselves faced with decided disadvantages. Our children, unhappily, suffer even more disadvantages than this. The 'free' dinner list shows that a large number of our children come from homes which are poor in the economic sense. Our own observations and the reports of the Welfare Committee show that many of our children come from homes that are poor in the moral sense. Almost all our children come from homes that are poor in the cultural sense. This adds up to the fact that we have to cater for over three hundred children, all of whom are under-privileged in the environmental and cultural sense and many who are decidedly under-privileged in the moral and economic sense as well. This is undoubtedly a tough assignment and will call for much energy, imagination and sympathy from all of us. If sometimes we become dispirited by our seeming lack of success, let us remember that the district has improved beyond all recognition, and we, by our effort, will certainly assist in the process of further improvement.'

In the past the school has been characterized by a high degree of mobility amongst the teaching staff and the present team of very young and very enthusiastic teachers all make long and expensive journeys to reach the school. (This is a real consideration when public transport is apt to be irregular, one is at the lower end of the salary scale, and there are teaching posts readily available in more pleasant surroundings nearer home.)

To work successfully with these children requires a high degree of skill and enormous patience, for not only do many of them lack the intellectual ability necessary for high academic success, but a high proportion have experienced emotional problems of such magnitude that learning presents additional difficulties. The majority of the children quite clearly need to be sure of love and affection before they can begin to untie themselves and make any educational progress. It is not always easy to ensure that kindness and gentleness are not mistaken for weakness, however. Having worked in this neighbourhood, I know something of the natural ruthlessness of these children towards the weak and ineffective teacher; life for such a person can be something of a torment. The school contains an odd mixture of the undersized, frail, big-eyed children and the sturdy, tough, aggressive youngsters presenting the inexperienced teacher with widely differing problems.

Despite this picture of almost unrelieved gloom, the school is an amazingly happy place to visit. The children certainly know how to laugh. They also know how to work, although the problems of working here are of quite a different nature to those in the first school. At no time have I seen a look of sullen defeat on any child's face but I have seen more looks of grim concentration and furrowed brows than in any other school I have ever visited especially in the remedial reading groups. Lacking in a rich vocabulary, these youngsters are great at conveying meanings by mime and gesture, and there is a traditional neighbourhood look which means 'I am involved in hard and complicated thinking'.

The standard of work produced by the children varies enormously. At its highest level it can equal the best of the work produced at the first school. But it would be wrong to compare them, for the situations are entirely different. (Nobody who saw the child crouching over a painting on the floor of the corridor would realize that he had been burnt by his father with a red hot poker and was legally 'in care'; the school undertakes the healing of scars of many kinds.) What can be compared is the interest and enthusiasm of the children, for both schools succeed admirably in sending on youngsters to the secondary stage of education who are eager to tackle any tasks seen to be worth while. Quite clearly both schools provide the opportunity for children to develop to their maximum ability. The chief difference is that they work in such contrasting surroundings and have such different starting points to education.

I found the third school the most exciting of all. Situated in the north of England in an isolated village, it was attended by 22 children of junior age and 13 of infant age. The headmistress herself taught all day, with an experienced assistant teacher taking the younger children. This meant that there were two qualified teachers working full-time with 35 children. Here was the richest work of all being attempted and achieved in the most delightful of all learning situations.

Although the school building was old, it was still remarkably spacious, and even with the whole school in one classroom for assembly there was nothing like the crowded atmosphere of the second school. There seemed to be all the time in the world for the children and teachers to talk together, to plan their work, to sort out their visits and excursions and to examine closely the things that were happening around them. Their art and craft showed a deep observation of the natural world, and the children's written reports and stories were superb.

Perhaps through a consciousness of their isolated situation, the teachers had made determined efforts not to be out of touch with current developments in primary education and as a result they showed themselves to be much better informed than a great many of their urban colleagues. With television in every home the children were as familiar with current programmes as city children, and their frequent discussions with the two adults gave the older ones a maturity that is not easy to achieve in more crowded classrooms. Doubtless these children lacked many of the advantages that come to children living in the larger towns. But they had also gained much that the others missed. Town children might be able to visit museums more easily, but at the time of my visit there were more than a dozen Greek vases and ornaments of the pre-Christian era being handled and examined by the children with perfect confidence. Together with a collection of African musical instruments these were on loan from the school museum lending service and were being put to good use.

It would seem that the efforts of the teachers and the enlightened local authority to ensure that these rural children were not too isolated in their primary education had resulted in them obtaining a most excellent start to life, and it certainly showed in the work that they were doing.

From: Arthur Razzell, *Juniors – A Postscript to Plowden* (Penguin Books, 1968).

This article is an attempt to show a less fortunate primary school in a slum area of a large city.

Geoffrey Lyons is Research Assistant in the Department of Education of the University College of Swansea.

DIFFICULTIES OF A
SLUM PRIMARY SCHOOL

A Wasteland

The school, standing on a steep hillside and reached by a long line of worn steps, occupies a typically grim Victorian building which it shares with a section of a technical college. Asphalt yards at the rear contain the toilets and a climbing frame. The immediate surroundings are a wasteland of demolished houses and of factories. The hillside has become a tip for scrap iron and disused furniture and is crowned by a ramshackle collection of hen pens and allotments. This is the children's natural playground and a constant source of friction between them and authority. To the front lies a busy main road, where one of the children had been knocked down by a car, and further to the rear are lines of back-to-back houses, the majority within five minutes' walk of school, where the children live. Sections of this area have been demolished, and the children moved school when the families were rehoused, but other families apparently move to another house in the same area and the children continue to attend the same school. Multi-storey blocks of flats are being built and the numbers of children on the school register should soon begin to increase. The school is a small one with approximately 110 children on the register and, therefore, only one unstreamed class per year.

The inside of the building was gloomy and grimy, the paintwork dirty and the walls stained with damp because the roof leaked. (The roof was damaged by people climbing on to it in the evenings.) The classrooms could hardly be described as bright and cheerful: they were cold in winter but full of the fumes of the leaky boiler. In Form Four's classroom, rows of old desks dominated the room: the walls, almost devoid of pictures or classwork, were peeling and filthy, and the bookcase, an antiquated glass-fronted cupboard, was perched precariously on two desks. Two other ancient cupboards stood on the floor and were stacked with dusty books, apparently published in 1933 or 1944, old clothes and mouse droppings.

The school had no facilities for cooking: meals were brought in containers from a central kitchen and served in the hall that also contained a limited amount of rarely used PE equipment. After school dinner, the dinner ladies swept the floor and then washed the dishes. The sinks were in Form One's classroom, the form teacher having apparently evolved some technique of coping with this.

The primary school and technical college did not exist happily together. There were constant complaints of missing property, books defaced, desks moved, chairs broken, after the technical college had occupied the rooms in the evenings. Similarly large day-release apprentices and primary school children could not coexist, simultaneously using the same playground for their breaks.

The teachers who had remained at the school for a period longer than one year had made a 'non-teaching' adjustment to the situation they faced daily. Apart from the headmaster, the staff were female and only one of them had been at the school longer than three years. None of them had any sort of qualification or training in remedial teaching, and since the educational system is linked to literacy this was a grave disadvantage. Nine children left the school last year unable to read or write anything but the most rudimentary English. (This is excluding immigrant children.)

The fourth year children had been without a class teacher for some time, the headmaster taking them himself, or relying on student teachers or other unqualified help.

The staff adopted extremely limited academic aims, if not abandoning them completely, and restructured their role to that of a social worker, in which they had little success either. They limited themselves to occasionally bringing cast-off clothes, baking bread and buying biscuits to sell to the children. They worked in the school, they said, because these children presented a challenge, they needed love and understanding. This was no insurance against the teachers having serious disciplinary problems, and lacking a knowledge of the basic techniques of dealing with children of this type, it is questionable whether the children received anything worthy of the name of education at all. But then the children's definition of what coming to school was about is far divorced from ideas normally current.

Playground Violence

There was a low school adaptation by the children. Their behaviour inside school was totally unrestrained and, in the playground, violent. The attitudes displayed towards education by both parents and children were in fact quite casual. A child would blandly arrive one morning and announce that he was 'coming to this school now'. A frequent reason for a change of schools were rows between parents and staff caused by what the parent judged as unfair treatment. Few parents visited the school, and those who did often arrived in a rage to complain. Absenteeism and truancy were rife; children were absent to run errands for mothers, aunties, the next-door neighbour, to look after a younger brother or sister, because mother was unwell, or even to have their hair done. Two boys absented themselves not only from school but from home as well and it was some days before the police, acting on information supplied by the children, effected a recapture. The other children found this quite amusing.

The police and children's welfare officers were in constant attendance. Every class in the school held a child with a police record, or someone in their family had a police record, or they had been before the court as being in need of care and protection. In one family the father had just been released from jail, in another family the father had just gone into jail, or hospital as his son euphemistically put it. Ten out of the 28 children in Form Four had a police record or belonged to a family that constituted a problem family. In Form Four three families were totally uncooperative to the school, not only at the level of refusing to allow their children to have medical treatment, or to go swimming, or if the school wanted their son to do PE then the school could supply him with PE kit, but in one case a legal battle was being fought to take the children from their parents and put them in a special home. An exactly similar case but with a different family was under way in Form Three. The headmaster, understandably, feared physical violence from one of the fathers. A large amount of the headmaster's time was in fact spent dealing with this sort of problem in order to ensure that his school continued as a functioning unit.

In the fourth form all the children's fathers with two exceptions (a shop assistant and a sales representative) were manual workers, and 12 of the 27 mothers had either a full-time or a part-time job. This hardly revealed the full picture. Two fathers quite clearly existed on the National Assistance Board, and in one case it was the mother who was the chief wage earner. In two (at least) of the families the father was the man who temporarily shared the mother's bed. Two sets of the parents had separated, the parents of one child were both aliens, one boy had a foster father, the mother having divorced and remarried. One boy's mother had died; his father was a night worker and therefore he spent much of his time with his grandparents.

Large Families

The families were large in size; out of the 28 children in Form Four, only three children lived in a family where there were less than three children, three children had five in their family, three had six, five had seven, and four children had eight brothers or sisters. In some of the families there was as much as 21 years between the eldest and youngest child and in two families of eight there were eleven years between the eldest and youngest.

Surprisingly, in view of this, only two children had free meals at the school, but perhaps this is because they lived so near to school. But in general money wasn't so short. Every family had a television set and only two did not own a washing machine; 15 of the 28 families said they owned a car, and one family had a motor cycle combination. Contrarily, the headmaster, knowing full well that some children never had a holiday away from home, arranged for six of the children to be provided with a holiday by a charitable institution.

The children's cultural horizons and experience were extremely narrow. Only one child ever read anything at home, and apart from two girls who claimed never to play out, watching television and playing out were the most popular spare time activities. None of them had heard of a town only five miles away, and there was one little girl who did not know that she lived in England. More understandably in this locality there were half a dozen children who had heard of spring but didn't have any understanding of what it was. One boy told me his mother woke him up at half past one last night to tell him she had won £35 on the bingo, 'but she only give me five lousy bob', and another boy wrote '. . . mum goes to get dad from the pub and then we have our dinner'.

Both parents and children subscribed to the idea that attendance at school was the equivalent of education, and there was a reluctance on the part of the children to do other than merely present themselves. There was a total unwillingness to integrate themselves into the school and adopt its aims and values; school was alien and extrinsic to them. The major activities were in the playground.

Pressure to Conform

The children, in contrast to most children of this age, never wanted to help in school, nor did they make school an extension of their lives by bringing into school something to show or to talk about. Certainly the most important school activity was playing out and in particular playing football. Here the more robust boys of the fourth year dominated the school, the lesser ones and younger children keeping out of the way and playing more childlike games, although of course all the seasonal games appeared in rotation. Only two or three boys (non-footballers) ever consistently joined in organized games with the girls, that is apart from chasing them or teasing them.

There was a considerably well developed 'group loyalty' between the children, to the detriment of the staff. The pressures towards conformity were strong, in particular not volunteering information about the frequent cases of bullying and pilfering that occurred. For example, the form teachers in two weeks lost 20 out of 30 brand new ball pens, even though the closest check was kept. Money was consistently stolen from the teachers' pockets. Three boys stole a pen and planted it on another boy in the class; they then informed the owner that they had seen X steal his pen. When he discovered his pen in X's coat, he and the other three beat up X. This was not reported but discovered by chance.

It is thought that children who have a low school adaptation will, for the boys, show this by being aggressive and disruptive; and for the girls, by being totally passive. Eleven of the 28 children unhesitatingly fitted into these two categories, four girls and seven boys. Whether in school or out of school a constant undercurrent of tension and hysteria was found that frequently spilled out into quite vicious fights between girls or boys, a pattern suggested by numerous anecdotes, common also at home. It was almost impossible to set the children work and expect them to do it, particularly when co-operation between two or more was involved. To attempt to compel a non-adapted type of child into something he didn't wish to do was always to run the risk of the child in a rage knocking over his chair or desk and storming out of the room to disappear for the rest of the morning, and frequently running home for his mother who would arrive at school shouting, screaming and hurling abuse.

Poor Health

Standards of health and hygiene were low. In Form Four seven children were classified as puny or appearing undernourished, five had had major illnesses – for example polio – or had been hospitalized for surgical treatment; two more were constantly absent through minor complaints; and five had speech defects (these five were educationally backward).

The general standard of hygiene was low. Five children in particular, including one girl, appeared regularly at school in a filthy condition, but granting the circumstances of their homes, where one cold tap was shared between seven, eight or nine, it wasn't so surprising. For some the only good wash was the compulsory shower before the weekly swimming lesson. Form Two, who didn't have a swimming lesson, were nevertheless sent for a shower each week. The school nurse confined two boys from the fourth year to their homes until the clinic certified they were free from head lice, and there was also an outbreak of fleas that proved immeasurably more difficult to localize, children finally coming with messages from their mothers that they hadn't to sit next to . . . The standard of dress was the feature that made the most immediate impact. I didn't realize that such children still existed: seven boys and one girl in the form came to school in what were rags and tatters, yet only one child had clothes supplied by the local authority.

Immigrants

To this school, as a result of an administrative reorganization, 26 immigrant children arrived one Monday morning, none of them speaking English or apparently able to speak to each other. Consequently and predictably one would be buttonholed by a mother demanding to know 'if this was going to be a black school' because 'if it is I want my kids out'.

The girls were more amenable to being in school; of only two of them could it be said that they made no effort whatsoever in class. By comparison this would apply to six of the boys. The general pattern was to do the minimum asked and only to work when specifically directed to. This applied to all but three of the pupils, two boys and one girl. The backward pupils in this atmosphere provided very serious problems to the teacher; in fact in such a setting it was impossible to deal with them effectively.

Whatever stimulation or incentive the teacher provided seemed to meet with the same failure. Their backwardness throughout their school careers had made them totally bored with school life and therefore a persistent and incurable disciplinary problem.

A Fresh Start?

In a general discussion of primary schools it is easy to overlook the existence of a school, as here described, where normal definitions are not applicable and a totally different treatment is necessary to cure its ills. The inevitability with which the circumstances add up to a school of this type is one of the more depressing features, under whatever heading one looks, the school is substandard. In its location, buildings and equipment, there is an urgent need of drastic change; most of the equipment – and in this it is sparse enough – needs to be thrown away and a fresh start made.

The school suffers particularly from a lack of young, able and energetic teachers. Unfortunately the type of teacher employed helps to contribute to the low standards because, unable to appreciate fully the situation with which she is faced, and also handicapped by a lack of the basic techniques of coping with this situation, a regressive effect is generated, the children becoming steadily more unmanageable as they become older.

One of the more serious factors that the teacher has to meet in the classroom is the ever present tension and the underlying instability of most of her pupils. Virtually all of them are in need of some sort of remedial education before what is normally considered as instruction can take place. Such a primary school without specially qualified staff is in fact without a central core of teachers who can go through the motions of teaching.

The school fails totally to present any challenge or enlightenment to help counteract this unfortunate environment. Already some of the children have police records and as they become older it seems inevitable that more of them will. It is not wished to exaggerate what a school can actually accomplish, particularly in an environment of this sort, but under these circumstances it would be desirable if the school did not reinforce the prevailing conditions quite so effectively.

But under whatever guise schools like this one are allowed to continue, they must remain a severe indictment of current educational practice, and of the level of public concern.

From: Geoffrey Lyons, 'Difficulties of a Slum Primary School', *New Society*, 14 Sept. 1966.

THE GRAMMAR SCHOOL

The challenge to the idea of segregated secondary education has led to considerable attention being paid to the nature of the grammar school.

This article gives a justification for the specialized type of education provided by such schools.

Robin Davis has been, since 1946, on the staff of Merchant Taylor's School, Northwood.

THE CASE FOR THE GRAMMAR SCHOOL

The approach of the grammar school is still, in the main, academic. Many of the subjects it teaches, though superficially useless, are of value in training the mind and developing personality. The demand for such trained minds in the adult world is fully established and steadily growing. For example the following is extracted from an advertisement for an intermediate post in a nationalized industry:

'The work requires clear thought, and eye for the relevant point, and the ability to draft quickly, in logical sequence and in plain English. . . .'

No mention here of particular knowledge or experience – indeed it is not clear, out of context, which nationalized industry is concerned, and it might well apply to any. Nor could one prescribe any one subject or course of training that would provide the qualities sought. The subject matters less than the approach, and this is, in effect, the academic approach, which broadly means treating a subject of little or no obvious practical value as tremendously important and worth while for its own sake. Now one of the hardest tasks of a teacher is to make a child on the threshold of secondary education see this. With some it is well nigh impossible, but it is easier with children of initial reading interest and ability, the prerequisite of which is usually a certain degree of intelligence and the consequence a readiness and desire to think and criticize for its own sake. The approach of the grammar school is therefore literary rather than practical – a 'sit down and think' school for 'sit down and think' children. One consequence of this is its apparently somewhat limited curriculum. Compared with the vast range of subjects offered at a large comprehensive school the grammar school resembles a one-man business competing with an educational supermarket. Yet paradoxically this is its strength. Offer a boy of eleven or thirteen a choice between commerce and Greek, or let a girl of similar age choose between typing and trigonometry and who can blame each, with their limited vision in a materialist world, for choosing the former option often enough, when they are 'first generation grammar school pupils', with their parents' blessing. For the 'sit down and think' child there is much to be said, on the long view, for such options as commerce and typing just not being available. Both choice of subject and standards of work are involved here. . . . In the words of a grammar school master, 'academically we drive, and only in the later years do the pupils realize why they have been driven'.

If the approach of the grammar school is academic to match the needs of the grammar school mind, its method of teaching is also distinctive. That this should be so is perhaps best seen by considering the different character of teaching in the modern schools. Here the approach is more graphic and often more imaginative and experimental than in grammar schools. Visual and other teaching aids are, or should be, more extensively used and there is need for the teachers to be more concerned with and enterprising in the presentation of their subject. As a comprehensive school headmaster put it 'they can't just preach, they really have to teach'. Now there is nothing wrong with preaching provided that you have an audience more or less prepared to listen, and here is the crux. By and large the grammar school child really does want to learn, though youthful pride would seldom admit it. But with the secondary modern child the teacher first has to persuade his class to want to learn before they can even begin to think about learning. Motivation must precede instruction, and often enough the former is a longer and more frustrating process than the latter. . . .

But if the grammar school approach to and method of learning is *different*, how far are we justified in suggesting that it is in some way *superior*? This word has two main uses: first, to convey that something is intrinsically better, and secondly, that it carries a higher status. Now things that are 'superior' in the first sense usually cost more, as when we speak of a 'Superior quality cloth'. In this sense a grammar school education is often more expensive in two ways. First, most of its staff and certainly a larger proportion than in a secondary modern school, are graduates, and this means the payment of graduate allowances and usually a more lavish scale of special responsibility posts. Secondly the pupil-teacher ratio in grammar schools is more favourable, on average 17–1 against 20–1 in modern schools. The average size of classes is roughly the same (28·4 and 28·6 respectively) but the larger sixth forms in grammar schools, with their smaller teaching groups, makes the overall ratio more favourable to them. But this is not always so and should not necessarily be so. For one thing, in many areas, as we have seen it is the secondary modern schools that have the new buildings and equipment, so that in terms of capital expenditure the balance has been redressed. . . .

But even where grammar school education does not cost more it is often regarded as 'superior' in some other sense. To some it may seem it is better absolutely. When we speak of an 'educated man' we usually think of someone who has had a grammar school type education. . . .

Values

The values of the grammar school are classless and inseparable from an academic education, and if the working class want those values, it is for them to come some of the way to meet them. And in honour to them many of them do. Neither of my own parents had more than a basic elementary education, and my grandparents were respectively a bricklayer and a farm labourer. I could have no help in the home with knowledge or cultural background for my grammar school course. But I did have, like many others, wisdom, understanding and encouragement. There was no resentment or criticism of my grammar school and its values – only an exaggerated and at times embarrassing deference. There is no reason why the 'working class', if we must use that term, should not be something more mobile than a rock in its relationship with the grammar schools – and in any case it is a rock which seems to be steadily disappearing. Why should it prove less capable of assimilating grammar school values than of acquiring a taste for consumer durables and holidays abroad, both hitherto regarded through economic necessity or social inertia, as the exclusive preserve of the middle and upper classes? To object to or seek to change grammar school values of one class is rather like going to France and objecting to the right-hand rule of the road or *priotité à droite* or feeling resentment because the French speak French. The British working class have enough sense and flexibility to recognize this. . . .

The case for the grammar school crystallizes into a case for educational efficiency. . . . There is such a thing as the 'grammar school mind' which the nation needs and other nations covet, and selection, for all the propaganda against it, is the best way so far devised to identify such minds and give them the kind of education that will develop their full potential. To call that education 'superior', though politically specious, is misleading; and to claim that the ethos of the grammar school conflicts with that of the working class is to make an out-of-date and class-obsessed generalization that is unfair both to the schools and to the working class itself. The traditional values and approach of the grammar school, despite plausible demands for modernization, are still relevant to the world of today. And, paradoxically, to preserve a system that appears to be socially divisive is the best road to educational efficiency, while social engineering through reorganization invites stagnation or decline.

From: Robin Davis, *The Grammar School* (Penguin Books, 1967).

The second extract taken from a study of 88 working-class children who completed a grammar school course reveals the difficulties some had in adjusting to the school and considers the conflict met by many working-class children between the values of the school and those of the neighbourhood.

GRAMMAR SCHOOL VALUES

Out of the children 48 spoke clearly of themselves as being identified with the school 'I was very much an establishment man. I was all establishment man!' whereas 15 were just as clear that they had declared *against* the school, and 25 held some intermediate position. Being *against* school did not necessarily mean being against school *work*. For all kinds of children, interest here was intense and success of supreme importance.

We pay a great deal of attention to the children who refused to accept the school. This is because we believe that they often represent the very large numbers of gifted working-class children who abandon grammar school at 16, and do not progress (as well they might) on to university and the professional life. Certainly the children we spoke to remembered large numbers of dissident pupils up to the fifth form, but few of these remained at school after this, and only a minority fall on our sample. The rebels left.

Who are the ones who *did* remain, and who especially are in this inner group of 15, who stand out uncompromisingly against the grammar school ethos? Five of the 15 come from 'sunken middle-class' homes; eight have fathers doing unskilled or semi-skilled work; 11 live in rented homes. Lightly sketched in like this we see that they come from all ranges of our sample, with perhaps a slight emphasis away from the very top reaches of the working class. . . .

The essential choice which these 88 children faced in the early grammar school years was one between school and neighbourhood. Some children had begun with few neighbourhood links, and for them this was no crisis. But the others who found themselves firmly, or sporadically, against the school were boys and girls who were still involved in neighbourhood life, and who preserved their other style of living. It was more than a matter of joining a youth club rather than the school scout troop; it had to do with deep differences in response, feeling, judgment – which recoiled against common images of 'dominance' or 'leadership': school uniform, teacher's gowns, prefects, the Honours Board, the First Eleven, the Scout Troop, the School Corps, Speech Day, Morning Assembly, Expected Public Decorum. The children who drew back from this spent their evenings in youth clubs, or with cycling groups or roaming the parks and streets in large inclusive gangs.

Their friendship, touching on middle-class children at school, centred around others in exactly their own situation and linked up with local children who had not passed the selection examination. Their basic loyalties were local loyalties. School was interesting and work was important, but for all that it was *only* 'Just where I went to learn things.' To the fuller social life it was hardly relevant. . . .

Meanwhile difficulties were arising within school. There was the school uniform. . . . The children who objected so strongly to school uniform were not the poorest children by any means. It seemed as if the objection was aimed at all those aspects of 'school' that did not have to do with 'work', but had to do with the school as an alternative community, as a particular code of living together and growing up. . . .

Almost any official side of the school was rejected by these children. They would not join the school corps, they would not join the school scouts. Nor would they even buy the school magazine. 'All the way down the school I'd refuse to buy the school magazine. I wasn't interested in buying it and I wasn't even interested in looking at it. I wasn't the only one, no. There were quite a bunch of us and the masters would come and bark at you and tell you how ashamed they were and how you were letting the side down, but I wouldn't buy it. And even when other kids bought it I wouldn't go and look at their copy.' It was odd to hear these consistent incidents in which children – often quite shy children – had taken a painful stand against the school over something which must have looked quite trivial to the teachers. Again it was not a case of the lack of money, though this might reinforce a stand, and it was not that the children could themselves explain why they were having nothing to do with this or that aspect of the grammar school. All they could say was, 'I won't,' and stick.

On the other hand, it was by no means clear that the school understood either, and often there was the sense of two strange worlds finding themselves side by side, yet with neither fully aware of the other's difference. Head teachers saw that some boys and girls retained neighbourhood links through youth clubs and similar bodies. Most tried to dissuade their pupils from membership. Speeches were made in assembly suggesting that youth clubs really belonged to secondary modern school children and should be left to them. For grammar school children there was the school community with its societies and homework. . . .

And daily from the teachers came a host of warnings, injunctions, suggestions, that spoke of the gulf existing. Working-class children felt themselves being separated from their kind. The choice between school and neighbourhood was faced daily in small concrete incidents. For the teachers these incidents were merely part of the pattern of manners, part of that training in 'tone' which distinguished the grammar school from the general community. They were honourably conceived and held, but for the child something much more central to his living was being locally but continually strained. 'She said you weren't allowed to eat ice-cream or sweets in the street. All sorts of silly things like that you'd have done *naturally*.'. . .

We recorded a lot of evidence about the school's insensitivity and the child's hypersensitivity; the school's determination to hand on the grammar school modes, to spread its standards as the best and the only standards, and the child's awkward, clumsy and stubborn desire to preserve the other ways, to remain 'natural'. This gaucherie soon moved into rudeness, tactlessness and the impolite.

From: Brian Jackson and Dennis Marsden, *Education and the Working Class* (R.K.P., 1962).

THE SECONDARY MODERN SCHOOL

R. Kneebone, headmaster of Beckfield County Secondary Modern School, York, outlines what he considers to be the aims and purposes of the secondary modern school.

TRIBUTE TO THE
SECONDARY MODERN SCHOOL

It would be true to say that no harder work and no more original thinking has been done anywhere than in secondary modern schools since their establishment just over ten years ago. It would be equally true to say that this has never been realized by the public. It is driving many secondary modern schools, mistakenly as I think, to seek recognition and esteem by creating within their schools examination streams and by entering pupils for external examinations.

We have a clear enough purpose. It is to take each child educationally as far as it can go – that means striving after true standards – and not neglect body and spirit. We do that, but because we have no examination results to show no other results can be seen. I will try to bring some of them within view of willing eyes.

Through the able work of our neighbouring primary schools the children who reach us are literate. Many are slow or even backward for the usual reasons of health, broken schooling, heredity and environment. They speak badly, read with little understanding, set their work down unintelligibly and resist attention. We work, as our primary school colleagues before us have done, to build confidence and win cooperation. We have our minor successes. Visitors tell us how well the children respond to questions and how eager they are to explain what they are doing or writing, even if it is not very good. With no other incentives than the highest – the desire to do their best for the children in our school – my teachers try every known method until at last there is something to build on. Suddenly a child who had no fluency in reading and writing finds himself able to do a little better and the improvement begins. There are those who say that these children should be turned out of school at fourteen to the labouring jobs for which alone they are fitted. That is not my view. Their work improves and so do they.

They are in our school during the most trying period of emotional and physical development in their lives. As we have had such a large proportion of children of secondary school age in our modern schools it stands to reason that we must expect most of the problems. Some of the children in difficulty because of emotional disturbance during adolescence have no strong support out of school and depend very much upon the care and help that we can give them. I have in mind several cases of children who were steered clear of juvenile court proceedings by the practical sympathy of teachers who made them work and gave them good advice. I can think of many cases of children with no training in courtesy or consideration who have learnt something of both before they have left us. The protection that we offer in school is continued with good effect in Junior Evening Schools and Youth Clubs. The public may think of secondary modern schools as breakwaters rather than lighthouses, but they should admit that because of us there are calmer waters ahead.

If we aim to improve work and behaviour we also offer our children the chance of acquiring a sense of responsibility. Senior pupils in grammar schools at 17 or 18 years will be prefects, captains of games or leaders of school societies. It would seem that the hierarchy in comprehensive schools will hardly come from the pupils leaving at fifteen. In the secondary modern school we have our opportunity and our pupils respond well to it. They are ready for responsibility and enjoy it, misusing their power sometimes but learning to assume care of a class or cloakroom with practice. They become smarter in appearance and walk with befitting dignity. They have a new sense of power in their developing physical condition; they have experienced using their authority in school games and clubs. We are in a position to tone down the over-exuberant and strengthen the nervous and uncertain. They are learning control over their speech, movement, opinions and feelings, each an education in itself. They are taking the first steps in self discipline. . . .

We demand the highest standard of work of which the children are capable. Seven out of every ten children leaving the primary schools continue their education in the secondary modern school. We take them as they are and try to help them to develop a right attitude to work, to people and to themselves.

Critics make rare play with our children's educational ability, with their behaviour, taste and manners. They exaggerate, of course, and their exaggerations fall on willing ears. We can say with truth that some of our children are the equal in what the public easily recognizes as educational ability of some children already benefiting from the prestige accorded grammar school education. We can say that in character, effort, bearing and disposition we have many children who will prove to be the decent citizens playing leading parts in factories, offices and shops. We have children of lower educational and social status who merit no less attention than any other child in any other kind of school. Only devoted service from our teachers can help with these children. . . .

It is my intention to pay tribute to secondary modern teachers in this and every school. No social prestige attends our efforts. New schools and new equipment have lent strength to our work, but our main strength must come from the spirit with which we approach our work and the belief that remains in us after years of hard striving in the face sometimes of ridicule and often of doubt.

We are preparing children not for examinations but for life. We teach facts. We seek to establish values. We work hard and long believing that what we are doing is as important in the fullest sense as teaching potential state scholars. We go to bed tired. We rise to face another day. We go into our morning assembly. We look around. Incentives? Here before us are five hundred incentives.

From: R. M. T. Kneebone, *I work in a Secondary Modern School* (Routledge & Kegan Paul, 1957).

This article describes the routine of a secondary modern school in a new well-equipped building. The author summarizes what he considers to be its chief defects.

John Partridge was a teacher in such a school and it now teaching educational sociology at a college of education.

SHORTCOMINGS IN THE SECONDARY MODERN SCHOOL

I do not think that anyone could say that Middle School was offering any kind of satisfactory education, from whatever point of view one chooses to define 'education'. How one views the life and work of this school depends, of course, upon one's basic assumptions. If one accepts the view that these are children of poor ability who are just incapable of serious work, who dislike school and play about because of their low intelligence quotients, who are best occupied playing sport or engaging in other non-academic activities, who are not of the material to rise out of their degrading lower-class habits and attitudes, and who are for all these reasons best sent out to work at an early age; then, perhaps, Middle-School style education is making the best of a bad job; it isn't too good, but after all it is the best that can be done with the material.

These are, sometimes, the attitudes of the teachers in Middle School. It's always education for someone else's children. One senior colleague said bluntly, 'Well, you wouldn't send your kid here, would you?'

However, there are some in Middle School whose basic assumptions differ from those of the pessimists, if so they can be called. These teachers recognize clearly how inadequate the education is, and how low the all-round standards in the school are. But they do not accept that this is inevitable and assert that all boys (and girls) are educable given the right encouragement and conditions. These men tend to see reform in political colours, claiming that the low standards in Middle School are due most importantly to the lack of adequate provision in the past for teacher training and general educational facilities. These are the kind of teachers who take their classroom teaching most seriously and who try to do their best for any 'D' or 'C' stream with which they are entrusted. Most admit that there is likely to be little improvement in either this type of education generally, or in their own personal lot, unless it is imposed from above by a Government with a different set of national priorities. Those who think along such lines may not be in a strong majority in Middle School, but at least they do differ in that they see improvement as possible in the near future.

Whatever the assumptions of the staff as to the nature and purpose and possible lines for improvement of the education proffered here, there is no disagreement about the low standards. In each 'D' class, there are boys who can neither read nor write; in the first-year 'D' class there may be fifteen who cannot, but by the time they have reached the third- and fourth-year classes, there may be only six or seven who still have a far below average reading age. I think it is fair to say that some five to ten per cent of each year group in Middle School are to all intents and purposes illiterate. In ascending order of literacy, the next group is a large one composed of the remainder of the 'D' boys and most of the 'C' boys. This large group have below average reading ages, but at least they can make sense out of simple prose, and show some progress during their three to four years in the school. But they will have difficulty in writing short letters or straightforward narratives; they tend not to be able to spell, neither to punctuate nor construct sentences. This means that some forty-five per cent or nearly half the boys here have not really acquired the essential tools for learning after between six and ten years at school. It hardly needs to be added that their grasp of any subject requiring literacy is inevitably poor.

A few boys in the 'C' stream, perhaps most of the 'B' stream, and the lower half of the 'A' stream, are boys who can read, in many cases well, and they are able to write comprehensible English. These boys may have mastered the tools of literacy, and of course they turn out some good work; some may be very good at certain subjects; there are those who show aptitude for woodwork or art, or for English composition. But the overall impression, however, is one of disinterest. These boys, who represent the most literate group of boys, bar one, in Middle School, seem steadily to lose interest the nearer draws the day for them to leave. The first- and second-year boys who belong in this group, and indeed most of the younger ones in all the streams show to some degree the natural inquisitiveness of children. But by the time they have reached the third year of their secondary education, they begin to worry about what they will do when they leave school; and because much of their school work appears to them irrelevant to this central concern in their lives, then they begin to lose any interest they might once have had in their classroom instruction. These boys are more articulate than their less literate fellows as well as more realistic about the limited range of opportunities open to them. These are the boys who want to get away from school and to get on with what seems to them to matter most – finding an agreeable, well-paid, interesting and secure job. These are the boys who say there would be no point in staying on at school until sixteen, because then they would have to compete with better educated Grammar school leavers of the same age who would get all the best jobs. These are sometimes the boys who are tempted to join the Forces as 'boy entrants' to learn a skilled trade. These are the boys who know what they want and seek the freedom, denied them at school, to wear tight jeans and pointed shoes, to grow their hair long and to listen to the Beatles.

Our most erudite boys are the ten or fifteen who compose the top half of the 'A' stream. These are the boys who do well in the Secondary Modern leaving certificate, who will pass certain subjects in the G.C.E. O-level examination, and for whose benefit much of the school time-table is designed. Some of them will go on to Technical Colleges or even Universities, but at the same time they leave Middle School too young to have acquired more than a basic grounding in certain narrowly defined subjects, and even as representing the best educated boys in this school they are not, perhaps, well fitted for the adult world.

From: John Partridge, *Life in a Secondary Modern School* (Victor Gollancz, 1966).

THE COMPREHENSIVE SCHOOL

In the first extract Margaret Cole, a prominent member of the Labour Party, outlines some of the arguments against the tripartite system of education and goes on to consider what should replace it.

THE CASE FOR THE COMPREHENSIVE SCHOOL

The Idea

We believe strongly that in a modern democratic community it is important, both socially and educationally, that children of all types shall learn to live with one another in youth; we believe that the advocates of 'segregated education', who would separate one or two or even five per cent of the nation's cleverest children at eleven years old and educate them apart from their fellows to become 'leaders', are making a great educational mistake. In the first place, there is no process known which can reliably separate out the cleverest children so young; in the second place, if they were so separated and separately taught so that they never came across the important fact that everyone (including themselves) is a duffer at something, the most likely end-product would not be great leaders but small boffins.

The idea of a comprehensive high school is that it shall cater for all children within a particular area from the age of eleven-plus to the time when they leave school, whether that be at fifteen, sixteen, seventeen, or whenever, except, of course, the handicapped children who need some form of special education, and the minority which will at present continue to go to the various kinds of independent and voluntary schools which still exist. For all the others – the great majority – children of all kinds, when they leave their primary schools, will enter the same high school.

This means that we deny the two assumptions on which most of the secondary education of today is based, that there are three types of child and three only – the grammar child, the technical child, and the modern child, of which the grammar child is the best. Anyone with any practical experience of children knows that both these assumptions are nonsense. There are not three 'types' of child but many types; and what we have to do, if we want to secure that every child receives the kind of education which best fits it for adult life and service to the community, is to see that courses of study are provided in schools which will bring out and develop every child's particular gifts.

From: Margaret Cole, *What is a Comprehensive School?* (London Labour Party, 1954).

Robin Pedley sets out the method of organization in a comprehensive school and outlines the advantages of this system.

He quotes research findings to illustrate the children's own attitudes to their respective schools – grammar, comprehensive or secondary modern.

Robin Pedley is Director of the Institute of Education at the University of Exeter.

INSIDE THE SCHOOLS

An English comprehensive school normally provides a 'foundation course' of either two or three years (ages eleven to thirteen or fourteen) which is followed by all pupils. The usual subjects are: English, mathematics, history, geography, art, handcrafts (boys), housecraft (girls), physical education, music, science, and religion. Religion is the only subject in the curriculum which *must* be provided. French, or another second language, is sometimes studied by all pupils, more often by all except the less able. Latin is usually begun by the more able pupils only.

I say 'less able' and 'more able' because it is the almost universal practice to group incoming pupils *on the base of general ability* so that the cleverest children learn together, and so on down the scale. This general-ability grouping, known as streaming, is usually done on the evidence of the eleven-plus examination, or where no such examination is now held in the district, on the children's performance at the primary school. Out of 102 comprehensive schools recently questioned on this subject, 88 stream the children on entry, 11 during or at the end of the first year. The remaining three do so after two years.

It should be noted that streaming is often in broad blocks rather than finely differentiating one class from another: thus a school which takes in 360 new pupils aged eleven, who have to be divided into twelve classes, may arrange them in four blocks graded A, B, C, and D, according to ability, with three parallel forms in each block. Fifteen of the 102 schools questioned have some classes of completely mixed ability, but only four carry such unstreamed classes beyond the third year, and these only in such subjects as crafts, art, music, religion, and physical education.

Further and more accurate grouping according to ability in particular subjects, known as setting, is usually confined to those pupils already placed in the top third or top half of their age group on general ability. Setting takes place mainly in mathematics, modern languages, English and science. About half the schools introduce it straightaway with the first-year pupils. Others wait till the second, third or fourth year. The constant rearrangement of pupils in different groups for different subjects which setting implies, means that it can only be used extensively in a big school with a lot of teachers.

From eleven to thirteen or fourteen then, there is something approaching a common curriculum in that the various subjects in the foundation course are taken by all or almost all the pupils. The ground covered in each subject, however, varies very widely between the top class and the bottom class of each age group. Individual children are moved up or down the scale according to their progress. The aim is to preserve and enhance the high standards of work which, it is claimed, result from grouping the pupils on ability, while removing the harmful effects, both scholastic and social, which are produced by enforced segregation in separate types of school. . . .

As children grow up, so their special aptitudes emerge more clearly. Pursuing its policy of giving an education suited to the needs of each pupil, the comprehensive school necessarily increases the number and character of different courses available to older pupils. This is done in two main stages. From thirteen or fourteen to sixteen the 'foundation' subjects are continued, but the time given to some of them is reduced, to others increased, to meet the special interests and needs of different children; and new subjects are introduced as required. The children begin to branch out in different directions, spreading wider as they grow to maturity. The diversity of subjects provided exceeds anything a normal grammar or 'modern' school can offer.

The final stage, for those who remain, is from sixteen to nineteen, called in England the 'sixth form'. Hitherto this stage of advanced study has been thought suitable only for that minority of boys and girls whose gifts are intellectual and academic. The comprehensive school certainly provides for them; but in addition it caters for the increasing number of pupils – whose ability may vary from great to small – who seek the benefit of extended secondary education. The number of examination subjects available at this stage is commonly therefore much greater than that provided by the average grammar school. Many comprehensive schools offer close on twenty subjects. For example, one school of 1,300 offers seventeen subjects, including Russian, Spanish, Law, Accountancy, and Technical Drawing. . . .

Eleven Plus 'failures'

Any selection process has very serious consequences for individual people. When I mention the following random examples of late development in our few comprehensive schools, I really have in mind the army of nameless ones who could have come up likewise but have been lost in the quick-sands of our selective system.

In 1961, 126 boys from the first comprehensive intake of 413 entered the sixth form of a London boys' school, sixty-two of them to study academic courses. These sixty-two came from no fewer than nine of the original thirteen first year forms – that is, some from well below the ability average as assessed at eleven. . . .

In a Home Counties school in 1961, four of the five university places obtained were won by boys who had failed the eleven-plus, and one of these won a State scholarship. . . .

At Bristol, 17 comprehensive school pupils who had failed the eleven-plus secured 26 advanced level passes among them in 1961. Six of them were accepted by universities, including one at Cambridge. . . .

(Examples of late development abound) – John, whose I.Q. was 91, gaining five G.C.E. passes at ordinary level: Jack, I.Q. 103, gaining six passes; Andrew, who came from the bottom stream of a central (intermediate) school passed advanced-level G.C.E. in history and mathematics, adding economics later, and now at university.

It would be tedious to go on. There is overwhelming evidence that the comprehensive schools are giving justice, in so far as that is possible, to children whose early progress has been held back. . . .

Children's Attitudes

How attractive and worth while does the comprehensive school seem to the pupils? . . .

Dr. T. W. G. Miller investigated pupils' attitudes and considered the question of values from their point of view.

Miller's study related to boys aged thirteen to fourteen. In three different parts of England he compared the attitudes of boys in grammar schools on certain matters with those of boys in comprehensive schools (termed comprehensive grammar below) whose abilities and home backgrounds were similiar. He likewise compared similar groups in modern and comprehensive schools (comprehensive modern below). His most significant conclusions were these:

1. The comprehensive grammar boys had a very slightly higher proportion of active leisure-time interests (e.g. playing rather than watching football) than the boys from separate grammar schools. Third came comprehensive modern groups, a bad last those from modern schools.

2. The group which had the highest opinion of its own school was comprehensive modern; second came comprehensive grammar, third grammar school, fourth modern school.

At the same time the boys' estimate of their school's standing in the eyes of the public was realistic: 1. grammar school; 2. comprehensive school; 3. modern school.

3. Comprehensive grammar and comprehensive modern together had the highest opinion of the *courses* offered by their schools. Grammar school and modern school came lower, and closer together.

4. Tests of 'morale' and attitude to schooling and education generally (e.g. homework) produced this order: comprehensive grammar closely followed by grammar school – the difference was scarcely significant; comprehensive modern; modern school.

5. Finally, all the boys were asked: 'Do you wish to leave school as soon as possible?' The answer 'No' came as follows: comprehensive grammar 93 per cent; grammar school 83 per cent; comprehensive modern 72 per cent; modern school 57 per cent.

Miller's work shows very clearly that the comprehensive schools are already meeting pupils' needs which in a divided secondary system are generally unsatisfied. It further shows that they are encouraging a bigger proportion to stay longer at school, learning to use their talents to the full. One of the most significant features of his findings is that even in the modern schools, where pupils clearly felt themselves and the school to be inferior, more than half wanted to continue their education. There is an enormous unsatisfied demand for higher secondary education.

From: Robin Pedley, *The Comprehensive School* (Penguin Books 1963).

NEW DIRECTIONS

The reorganization of secondary education has continued and there is considerable variety of provision among the local authorities.

One experiment tried by a number of schools, particularly at primary level, was the unstreaming of classes. Brian Jackson's study of the social effects of streaming in 10 streamed and 10 unstreamed primary schools is here examined.

THE STREAMED AND
UNSTREAMED SCHOOLS

A Comparison

Some of the 'A' classes seemed particularly excellent in almost every respect, but few of the schools were successful with their 'B' or 'C' classes. Often the 'C' class was low in attainment, and markedly demoralized: possibly its very classroom was separated from the school proper. 'A' classes were in the charge of older, more experienced teachers. Nine out of the ten deputy heads taught 'A' streams. Heads were often uneasy about this and in favour of a transfer of teachers and pupils from class to class, but such transfer was never great because of the gap that opened up between 'A', 'B', or 'C' pupils and because strong teachers established in key 'A' stream posts were hard to budge. These ten schools, selected gifted children early and divided their pupils up into three broad kinds of ability. The future academics, craftsmen, and labourers whom it produced kept their own 'stream', but within that developed their approved talents more thoroughly.

Compared to the ten streamed schools, the unstreamed sample were mostly new schools or schools in working-class areas. In order to flourish, 11 plus selection had to slacken or disappear, and pressure from parents to be minimal. On the whole they sent a smaller percentage of children to grammar school, but were cited in areas which had a smaller percentage of grammar schools anyway. Two of the Heads did not allow a full survey of their school. The remaining eight schools were, as a group, more crowded yet more relaxed in atmosphere than the streamed schools. There was not the drive, competition or tension common in the streamed schools; more time was was devoted to music, art and drama, and rather less to the desk work of arithmetic and English exercises. It was hard to compare the two groups of schools, since so much more than unstreaming distinguished them. The teaching techniques were usually different – with less class work, and much more small group and individual work. They were schools in which children frequently *surprised* their teachers by some new interest or success. Because there was a difference of values, techniques, expectation and organization between the two types of school, academic comparisons are difficult to judge. Furthermore, the school records were sometimes of doubtful value. Allowing this, there were eight cases where the reading progress of a year group of streamed children could be compared with a year group of unstreamed children. Two of these comparisons showed little difference between either method. The other six keep to the following pattern: all children improved somewhat in the unstreamed schools, but the weakest children gained most. Besides creating higher academic standards, unstreamed schools had a narrower spread of attainment. The long 'C' stream tail had disppeared.

Before making these comparisons I was already doubtful of the value of streaming, though impressed by the vigour which sometimes went into a classic streamed school. I had little experience of large, unstreamed schools, though I had liked the free and friendly atmosphere I had known in schools too small to consider streaming. By the end of this survey several personal impressions had clarified. First, though an academic comparison between the two systems now seems to me to be extremely subtle and full of pitfalls, I think there are reasonable pointers suggesting that unstreaming can abolish the 'C' stream tail. It may be that otherwise there is academically little difference between the two methods.

But there certainly were considerable *social* differences between them. I did not know how to measure atmosphere or mood but I record as an impression that unstreamed schools replaced competition by helpfulness, and had re-created in large schools the friendly atmosphere I noted in small ones. For example, in most of the streamed schools it was an offence for one child to turn to another for aid with an arithmetical problem. This was 'copying' and to be punished. Yet in most of the unstreamed schools this turning of one child to another was constantly encouraged by the teachers and rewarded with small words of praise. I never spoke to a child who had moved from a streamed to an unstreamed school but I imagine it could be an astonishing experience.

Not only the system changes, but the importance of certain lessons, the very position where the teacher stands in class, the relationship of child to child, the whole ethic of the room.

This was the social difference as the child met it. But to the adult observer the main distinction lay in the development of children's gifts. Streamed schools produced a predetermined number of gifted children: the kind of giftedness they encouraged was also predetermined. But the unstreamed schools were less predictable, more varied. They were schools in which children surprised teachers. This summary is perhaps too generous to their many small faults; but at their best moments unstreamed schools drew *more* of the child into classroom activity and helped bring into life the multiplicity, the often odd mixtures of abilities that boys and girls had in them.

I was impressed by many of the achievements of streamed schools that I saw, and did not feel that the comparisons made here were between ten *bad* schools and ten *good* ones. But I was more impressed by the *potentiality* of the unstreamed schools. There were schools in which, at their finest, there were few bars to the amount or kind of excellence that they nurtured. The streamed schools were like magnificent machines able to refine precisely limited amounts of gold, silver and baser metals. But the unstreamed schools had the potentialities of yeast which, under good conditions, reduplicates.

From: Brian Jackson, *Streaming: an education system in miniature* (R.K.P., 1964).

Several authorities are experimenting with changes in the age of transfer from junior to secondary schools.

Alec Clegg, Director of Education in the West Riding of Yorkshire, explains the reasons for establishing a Middle School.

In the second extract a chief inspector for primary and secondary schools at the Department of Education and Science tries to define the task of middle schools.

THE MIDDLE SCHOOL (1)

In one suggestion for the reorganization of secondary education proposals include a fundamental change, in that the 'normal' age of transfer from primary to secondary school at about the age of eleven is disregarded, and new kinds of school are envisaged which will have within them children who under present arrangements are of both primary and secondary school age.

In many parts of the country these are coming to be known as 'middle schools' and in the case of the West Riding Authority the majority of these will cater for children aged about nine to about thirteen. . . .

The reasons which led to the selection of this age-group rather than other possibilities were both educational and organizational. It was felt that any break later than thirteen was undesirable, since this would leave too short a period in which the high school could prepare its pupils for the leaving examination at sixteen. Given, however, this three-year run in the high school to the leaving examination, the majority of those head teachers who were consulted pointed out that the middle school would not have to concern itself with examination pressures too directly and would be able to provide an education related to the needs and interests of the children at that stage in their lives. Many head teachers pointed out that it is precisely at this time – towards the end of the second and the beginning of the third year in the secondary school – that they and their staffs notice changes taking place in the attitudes and interests of children in their school, and that in many small but significant ways secondary schools do recognize some sort of break at this stage.

Having selected thirteen as an appropriate point for the upper limit of a middle school, a decision had to be made about the lower limit. A three-year span was the minimum which could be considered, since the suggestion of a two-year school, in which every child is either a new entrant or a leaver, was felt to be unacceptable. Four years was generally agreed to be better than three, and a number of primary school head teachers advised that by the age of nine the majority of children have gained sufficient mastery of the basic skills to be able to use them without difficulty in the development of their experience and understanding.

From: Alec Clegg, 'The Middle School Cometh', *The Teacher* (1967).

THE MIDDLE SCHOOL (2)

The middle school will have its roots in our primary schools, the traditions and the strengths of which we must retain. Foremost among these may be reckoned the quality of personal relationships; the variety of stimuli which prompt children to observe, discover and learn through their own experience; the consequent range and diversity (sometimes staggering in its variety) of activities, topics and interests in which the children engage; and the stress on matching both work and pace to individual capacities and needs. Some would claim that the opportunity to extend these approaches and attitudes for a further two years would justify middle schools, apart from any other gain; and that the slower and less confident children in particular will benefit is almost beyond doubt. Yet to overlook the contributions of the secondary school to the education of the eager young teenager (for such the oldest pupils will be) would be to neglect much of great value.

Foremost among the contributions of the secondary school are the introduction to disciplined study and to the need for precision in observation, calculation, language and thought; the systematic and orderly extension of knowledge in a subject or a field; the formation of specific individual tastes and aptitudes after the widely roving period of exploration in the junior school; and the development of such personal attributes as the ability to make objective judgments and responsible choices. The task before the middle school is to create teaching and learning situations in which pupils pass gradually and naturally into these more adult stages, maturing at their own best pace; to establish the continuity of the educational process, making a bridge between primary and secondary, dominated by neither.

From: L. J. Burrows, 'What's in Store for the Children?' *The Teacher* (1967).

Leicestershire proposed a different solution to the problems of organizing secondary schools. In 1963 the Director of Education outlined the plan which has been followed in parts of the country.

THE LEICESTERSHIRE PLAN

The Leicestershire experiment proposes a system in which the grammar school is associated with a number of secondary modern schools to form a single educational unit. All pupils would enter the appropriate secondary modern school and would be taught there for the first three years of the secondary course. At the end of the third year of the secondary course, transfer to the grammar schools would be open to all children whose parents were prepared to give an undertaking that they would leave them at school for an extended course at least up to the end of the school year in which they attain the age of 16. The remaining children would stay in the secondary modern school until they reach leaving age at 15, although they would be encouraged, for example with the aid of suitable vocational courses, to stay at least until the end of their fourth year.

This reorganization obviously involves some changes in the functions of the two types of school. The modern school will have to provide from the outset a curriculum suitable for children who are to proceed to an advanced course. It will, for example, have to offer a second language and possibly at some point Latin. At the other end, the grammar school will have to provide suitable courses of a technical or semi-vocational kind for children whose parents wish them to follow an extended course but who would not be suited to the requirements of the Ordinary and Advanced levels of the General Certificate of Education. Indeed, it is a point to note that any pupil, whatever his level of intelligence, is eligible to go forward to the next stage of education provided he is prepared to stay at school long enough to justify it. . . .

The Headmaster of one of the Leicestershire Plan upper schools wrote in the autumn term 1962 some notes of his impressions for a team of visitors. With his permission I quote the following extracts:

Academic Standards

'The commonest criticism levelled against the Leicestershire Plan is that academic standards are bound to drop. Nobody has, to my knowledge, adduced any evidence in support of this claim – and indeed with the best will in the world such evidence would be extremely difficult to provide. The claim is based upon a much more insidious "feeling" that such is the case.

'One can only answer such a "feeling" by a conviction based on living in the school and watching pupils develop intellectually. I do not believe that any of our best academic pupils would have done any better in any other school and I am quite sure that large numbers of pupils have done much better under this scheme than they would have done elsewhere.'

The Problem of Integration

'How, it is asked, is it possible to make pupils feel a part of the school when they are with you in many cases for only two years, from fourteen to sixteen? The answer to this has, I think, been provided this term. We had considered that there might be a problem but that it would not arise really until the intake of September 1962. Always, before that, there had been in the school a nucleus of the same age group – the $12\frac{1}{2}$ per cent which had come at eleven. We had regarded these three forms as having a binding effect on the intakes – able to show them the ropes and help them to settle down quickly. But in September 1962 the whole fourth year would be new and there would be none of their contemporaries to meet them in, for the last eleven plus intake would now be fifth formers.

'Already this term we are convinced that the nucleus of previous years, far from having an integrating influence, was in fact an irritant, for the new intake this term is quite different from that of previous years. They are relaxed, enthusiastic and eager and have settled down remarkably. They have flocked to join school societies and have made us feel that they are completely at home and a part of the school in a very real sense. They realize that some of them are brighter than others but it worries none of them because they have been together in many cases from the infant school, and there has been no segregation at any time apart from the fact that they were in different forms – as they are now.'

Recruitment of Staff

'It is commonly supposed that a school such as this, with its wide range, experiences difficulty in recruiting staff with adequate qualifications. Experience has proved exactly the opposite. Every single year since the school came into existence additional staff have had to be appointed and apart from the difficulties which every school experiences in recruiting Mathematics and P.E. mistresses – there has always been a good field to choose from. I have always provided the fullest information to candidates about the general set-up of the school and always, having done this and before interviewing candidates individually I have invited them to withdraw if they so desired. No candidate has ever done so.'

An Adult Community

'I am quite sure that a school with an age range of 14–19 has distinct advantages over one in which the range is 11–19. My experience is that in the latter school because of the presence of 11, 12 and 13 year olds, the regime tends to become authoritarian, and it is not until the sixth form that emancipation takes place.

'The effect of making a change of school at fourteen, when other changes – both physiological and physchological – are also taking place is that a new impetus is given to work and every other branch of school life. We do not experience that sag in enthusiasm and interest which occurs so often at the end of the third year in a normal grammar school and which tends to make the fourth year such a problem. On the contrary our fourth year intakes come into an atmosphere of serious work and display much of the brightness and enthusiasm that the eleven year olds display on entering a grammar school.

'It is possible, therefore, to treat the whole school as a much more adult community and this we try to do in the expectation that the pupils will respond in an adult way. It is possible to extend much farther down the school that relationship between pupil and teacher which one expects to find between best sixth forms and staff – in fact an adult relationship.

'Living with it all the time one is perhaps not the best judge of how far this has yet been achieved but new members of staff and many visitors to the school volunteer their opinion that it has certainly begun.'
From: Stewart C. Mason, *The Leicestershire Experiment and Plan* (Council and Education Press, 1963).

Finally, an article in *The Observer* gives a vivid glimpse of the direction in which the schools of the future may be moving.

A SCHOOL OF THE FUTURE

This projection of how schools might work is based on one important premise: that schoolchildren, given the right atmosphere, equipment and upbringing, will work on their own. This already happens in a handful of schools.

The school's hub a huge resources centre. Here, the children may spend almost half their day. There are books, and places to read them. Television, both live and on videotape. Filmstrip, and back-projection screens. Teaching machines and programmes, language-learning equipment. Links with the teaching computer (perhaps a regional one serving several schools): each child dials his code number and the computer will start where he left off last time. And, of course, grownups to help children when they need it.

The resources centre is quiet. It's built to baffle sound, with carpets and sound absorbent materials. And if children want to make a noise they have a common room with a coffee bar and pop music and anarchy.

Near the resources centre there are seminar rooms where teachers can take small groups of children. There's the school's closed-circuit television studio where both teachers and children make programmes. The teachers have their own common room, and offices where they can work and plan.

The children who aren't working in the central block are out in the specialized buildings. In the science and technology centre, with its labs and workshops, they're doing practical work – perhaps on their own, sent there from the resources centre by a computer programme, perhaps with a teacher. The social studies block is the headquarters of teachers of history, classics, literature, language and social sciences, with the special equipment and teaching space they need.

There's a centre for music and drama, and another for arts and crafts: these, and the science centre, spill out into covered outdoor patios to make more space for big or noisy work. There's a huge sportsdrome. And there's a cafeterium, mainly for self-service lunches, but also equipped for big school functions.

The key to the whole operation is computer time-tabling. By computer, you can quickly work out an individual timetable for every teacher and student in the school, allocating times for use of the specialist places, and for things like lunch.

From: *The Observer*, 2 July 1967.

INDEX

ABILITY
  waste of 29–33, 33–34, 34–37
ACHIEVEMENT
  determinants of 25–27, 28, 29–33,
    34, 34–37, 38–39, 43–45, 46–47,
    47–50, 58–59, 61–63, 63–65
ACCOMMODATION
  for schools 51–52, 53–57, 69–73,
    73–79, 111
ACTS OF PARLIAMENT
  see education acts
ADOLESCENTS
  problem of proper educational
    treatment of 7, 8–10, 81–83,
    88–90, 94–95
AGE OF ENTRY TO SCHOOL
  60–61

BERNSTEIN, BASIL 47–49
BOARD OF EDUCATION 4

CAPITAL INVESTMENT 3,
  19–21
CASE FOR PUBLIC
  EDUCATION 3
CENTRAL SCHOOLS 7
CHILDREN
  interests of 8–10, 39–42, 69–73,
    81–84, 88–90
CHURCH SCHOOLS 3–4
CIRCULARS OF BOARD OF
  EDUCATION
  Educational Reconstruction 1943
    10–14
  10/65 14–16
CODE
  elaborate 47–49
  restricted 47–49

COMMUNITY
  school as 16, 83–87, 103–105,
    108–110
COMPREHENSIVE SCHOOLS
  organization of 14–16, 95–97
  type of education 14, 94–95
CURRICULUM 3, 8–10, 12, 81–84

EARLY LEAVING REPORT
  29–33, 43–45
EDUCATION ACT
  1870 3
  1902 4, 12
  1918 4
  1944 10
EDUCATIONAL PROVISION
  history of 3–4, 5–7
  regional variation in 61–63
  structure of 10–14, 14–16
EDUCATIONAL
  RECONSTRUCTION 1943
  10–14
ELEMENTARY SCHOOLS 39
ELEVEN PLUS 4, 10–14, 14–16,
  28, 36, 39, 61–63
ENVIRONMENT
  influence of 51–52, 53–57, 69–73,
    74–80
EXAMINATIONS 12
EXPENDITURE
  government 3, 19–21
EXPERIMENT 103–105, 105–107,
  108–110, 111

FAMILY
  attitudes of 38–39, 40–42, 43–45,
    58–59, 74–80
  size of 45–47, 77

FAMILY—*cont.*
   social class of 25–27, 28, 29–33,
      33, 34–37, 38–39
"FILL THE GAPS" 3
FINANCE 3, 19–21
FISHER, H. A. L. 4

GIRLS
   education of 44
GOVERNMENT REPORTS
   see Early Leaving Report, Hadow
      Report, Newsom Report,
      Norwood Report, Plowden
      Report, Robbins Report
GRAMMAR SCHOOL
   type of education 8, 12, 81–84
   provision of places 28, 62–63
   and social class 28, 29–33, 40–42
   values 83, 84–87

HADOW REPORT 6
HEALTH 78
HIGHER EDUCATION 33–37
HIGH SCHOOLS 4
HIGHER TOPS 3

IMMIGRANTS 79
INDIVIDUAL
   needs of 4, 12, 13, 81–83, 88–90

LANGUAGE 47–50
LEICESTERSHIRE PLAN 108–9
LIVING CONDITIONS
   effect of 37–39, 58–59, 74–80

MIDDLE SCHOOL 105–106, 107

NATIONAL INCOME 21
NEIGHBOURHOOD
   and school 51–52, 53–57, 74–80
NEWSOM REPORT 53–57
NORWOOD REPORT 8
NUTRITION 79
NURSERY SCHOOLS 11

OBJECTIVES OF EDUCATION
   5–6, 7, 13–14, 19–21

OPPORTUNITY IN
   EDUCATION 25–27, 28,
      29–33, 33–37, 46–47, 60–61,
      61–63, 63–65

PARENTS
   attitudes to 43–45
   school leaving interests 38–39,
      40–42
   social classification 25–27, 28,
      29–33, 33, 34–37, 38–39, 47–50
PLOWDEN REPORT 51, 60–61
POVERTY 74–79
PRIMARY SCHOOLS 4, 11,
   25–27, 38–39, 51–52, 60–61,
   63–65, 69–73, 74–80

RESOURCE CENTRES 111
ROBBINS REPORT 33–37

SCHOOL
   as community 16, 83–87
SCHOOLS
   see nursery, primary, grammar,
      secondary modern,
      comprehensive, middle schools
SCHOOL BOARDS 3
SCHOOL CLASS 25–27
SCHOOL LEAVING 4, 10, 37,
   40–42, 43–45
SECONDARY MODERN
   SCHOOLS
   type of education 9, 12–13, 53–57,
      88–89, 90–93, 107
SELECTION 4, 10–14, 14–16, 28,
   35, 36, 39, 61–63
SEX
   and school leaving 44
SOCIAL CLASS
   effect on educational achievement
      25–27, 28, 29–33, 33, 34–37,
      38–39, 40–42, 43–45, 46–47,
      48–50, 63–65, 84–87
SOCIETY
   needs of 5, 12
STREAMING 25–27, 63–65,
   103–105

TEACHERS
    assessment of children's ability
      64–75
    availability 55–57, 69, 74–80
    views on home influences 25–27,
      38–39
TECHNICAL SCHOOLS 9, 13
TRIPARTITE SYSTEM
    justification of 8
    structure of 11–14

UNIVERSITY
    entry 33

VALUES 83, 84–87, 91, 94–95,
    97–99

WASTE OF ABILITY 29–33,
    33–34, 34–37